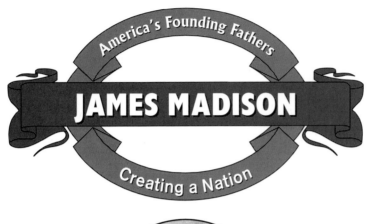

America's Founding Fathers

JAMES MADISON

Creating a Nation

Zachary Kent

Enslow Publishers, Inc.

40 Industrial Road   PO Box 38
Box 398   Aldershot
Berkeley Heights, NJ 07922   Hants GU12 6BP
USA   UK

http://www.enslow.com

Library of Congress Cataloging-in-Publication Data

Kent, Zachary.
        James Madison : creating a nation / Zachary Kent.
            v. cm.—(America's founding fathers)
        Includes bibliographical references and index.
        Contents: The fight for the Constitution—Young revolutionary—
Designing a national government—United States congressman—
Secretary of state—The fourth President—Mr. Madison's war—
Defeat and victory—The father of the Constitution—Timeline.
        ISBN 0-7660-2180-7
        1. Madison, James, 1751–1836—Juvenile literature. 2. Presidents—
United States—Biography—Juvenile literature. [1. Madison, James,
1751–1836. 2. Presidents.] I. Title. II. Series.
E342.K45 2004
973.5′1′092—dc21

                                        2003011483

Printed in the United States of America

10 9 8 7 6 5 4 3 2 1

To Our Readers: We have done our best to make sure all Internet addresses in
this book were active and appropriate when we went to press. However, the author
and the publisher have no control over and assume no liability for the material
available on those Internet sites or on other Web sites they may link to. Any comments or suggestions can be sent by e-mail to comments@enslow.com or to the
address on the back cover.

Illustration Credits: Clipart.com, pp. 42, 72, 79, 102, 105, 108; Enslow
Publishers, Inc., pp. 15, 59; Library of Congress, pp. 13, 19, 21, 22, 34,
36, 47, 52, 57, 61, 71, 77, 82, 91, 101, 106, 111; National Archives,
pp. 2–3, 4–5, 7, 10, 28, 45, 68, 76, 81, 96, 112–113; June Ponte, p. 1.

Cover Illustration: Corel Corporation (background); June Ponte
(portrait).

Contents

After the surrender at Yorktown in 1781 the Peace Ball was held in Virginia. In a few years America won its independence from Great Britain with the Treaty of Paris which was signed in 1783.

The Fight for the Constitution

"THE PLOT THICKENS FAST," George Washington declared, "a few short weeks will determine the political fate of America."[1] He wrote these words in May 1788 to his French friend the Marquis de Lafayette, who had helped Washington's army during the Revolutionary War. With the signing of the Treaty of Paris in 1783, the United States had won its independence from Great Britain. In the summer of 1787, delegates from twelve of the thirteen states met in Philadelphia, Pennsylvania. Together, these delegates designed a strong new government for the nation. The set of laws they wrote was called the Constitution.

The Importance of Virginia

The convention delegates decided that at least nine of the thirteen states had to ratify the Constitution. This meant that nine states had to approve the document for it to be accepted. By June 1788, eight states had voted to ratify: Delaware, Pennsylvania, New Jersey, Georgia, Connecticut, Massachusetts, Maryland, and South Carolina. One more state was needed.

Virginia was the largest of the thirteen states in both size and population. Virginians suddenly found themselves in a very important position. It seemed that the success of the Constitution depended on Virginia becoming the ninth state to ratify. If Virginia rejected the document, the future of the entire country might be affected.

Not everyone in Virginia favored the strong national government called for by the Constitution. Patrick Henry was a Virginia patriot. In 1775, Henry had declared the famous words, "I know not what course others may take; but as for me, give me liberty or give me death."[2] But Henry wanted state governments to be more powerful than the national government. In a speech to the Constitutional Convention, Henry declared, "There will be no checks, no real balances, in this government."[3] He worried that a strong national government would crush the liberties of the states. Henry's speeches made acceptance of the Constitution very uncertain in Virginia.

Among the Virginians in favor of the Constitution, one man took the lead. Thirty-seven-year-old James Madison was a small, soft-spoken man. But Madison had a brilliant mind. Alexander Hamilton of New York wrote to him, "Our only chance of success depends upon you."[4]

The Virginia Ratification Convention

Delegates to Virginia's ratification convention gathered in Richmond, Virginia, on June 2, 1788. Madison stood and spoke to them for the first time. Hugh Blair Grigsby described him: "His [small size] made it difficult for him to be seen from all parts of the [room]; his voice was rarely loud enough to be heard throughout the hall. He . . . rose to speak as if with a view of expressing some thought that had [just] occurred to him, with his hat in his hand and his notes in his hat . . ."[5]

Patrick Henry was famous for his dramatic speaking style. Here, Henry's famous words, "give me liberty or give me death" are delivered to the Virginia Provincial Convention in 1775.

In the days of debate that followed, delegates found Patrick Henry's comments very entertaining. Henry used dramatic gestures and pauses when he spoke. For his part, Madison presented calm, intelligent arguments. Replying to Henry on June 6, Madison declared, "Let the dangers which this system is supposed to be replete with be clearly pointed out: if any dangerous and unnecessary powers be given to the general legislature, let them be plainly demonstrated, and let us not rest satisfied with general assertions of danger, without examination."[6]

Madison's speeches were full of force, reason, and truth. He compared the strong government designed by the Constitution with the governments of ancient Greece and modern European nations. Throughout history, he warned, governments without energy or strength had always failed. A convention reporter wrote down everything that was said during the debates. He made notes such as "Here Mr. Madison spoke so low that he could not be heard."[7] Many times, interested delegates left their seats and pressed close around Madison in order to hear his words.

Keeping Up the Fight

After one tiring debate, Madison fell ill. For the next four days, he remained in bed with fever. But at last he rose to continue the fight. He gave his last important speech on June 22. He asked his listeners to consider "whether thirteen states shall unite freely . . . for security of their common happiness and liberty, or whether every thing is to be put in confusion and disorder."[8]

On June 25, 1788, the moment at last arrived for the Virginia delegates to vote. It was a close decision. But the convention approved the Constitution, 89 to 79. The Constitution was now guaranteed to become the new law of the nation.

Virginians realized the success of the Constitution in their state was due to Madison. The brilliant man with the weak voice had beaten the great public speaker Patrick Henry. Although they did not know it, New Hampshire already had ratified the Constitution on June 21, the ninth state to ratify. By August 1788, eleven states had ratified, and in the end, Rhode Island and North Carolina would also agree. The great contest for the Constitution had been won. French visitor J. P. Brissot de Warville wrote of Madison: "He has rendered the greatest services to Virginia, to the American Confederation, and to liberty and humanity in general. . . . Mr. Madison won the members to it by his eloquence and his logic."[9]

The Founding Fathers

James Madison belongs to a special group of Americans that has come to be remembered as the founding fathers. During the 1770s and 1780s, this group created a new and independent nation, the United States of America. The creation of the United States was a revolution. It seemed to turn the entire world upside down. It established the idea that all men had rights.

The founding fathers were average people: lawyers, farmers, doctors, and merchants. They made great personal sacrifices to establish their dream of democracy in America. They defied Great Britain's King George III and risked their lives signing the Declaration of Independence. After that, England regarded them as rebels and traitors. They remained true to their revolutionary cause through eight hard years of war. And when the fighting ended, they boldly designed the Constitution. This document remains today the foundation of the United States national government. With the passage of time, the founding fathers have become legendary American heroes. Taken together, they are a symbol of the greatness, wisdom, and courage it took to form the United States.

James Madison's powerful speeches helped get the Constitution ratified in Virginia.

James Madison certainly earned his place as a member of that historic group. His contributions to the writing and ratification of the Constitution earned him the title "Father of the Constitution." His influence was extremely important in getting the Constitution accepted by the states. As a congressman, Madison almost single-handedly saw that the first ten amendments to the Constitution were passed. They are known today as the Bill of Rights. As fourth President of the United States, he held the nation together during the War of 1812. James Madison lived his entire adult life devoted to the United States. In 1836, Kentucky Senator Henry Clay declared, "Mr. Madison rendered more important services to his country than any other man, Washington only excepted."[10]

Young Revolutionary

JAMES MADISON, JR., was born at midnight on March 16, 1751. He was born at his grandmother's house near what is now Port Conway, Virginia. His mother, Nelly "Eleanor" Conway Madison, felt more comfortable having her first baby at her mother's home. Her husband, James Madison, Sr., owned a large tobacco plantation in Orange County, Virginia. He was one of the richest men in the region. He also served as a justice of the peace and was commander of the local militia, which was the volunteer army company.

From Mount Pleasant to Montpelier

In the years that followed, eleven other children were born to James and Nelly Madison. Sadly, five died of illness while still babies. But James Madison, Jr., grew up with six healthy brothers and sisters: Francis, Ambrose, Nelly, William, Sarah, and Frances.

The family gave young James the nickname of "Jemmy." He was not a strong boy and often fell sick. But when he was able, he played with his brothers and sisters. He learned how to ride horseback and enjoyed exploring the neighborhood woods and fields.

The Madisons lived in a simple wooden house on the plantation called Mount Pleasant. Around 1760, James's father decided to build a larger

Nelly "Eleanor" Conway Madison and James Madison, Sr., had eleven children together, including James Madison.

house a quarter mile north of the old house. Carpenters and bricklayers went to work. The new house was a two-story brick mansion. It stretched eighty feet across the front. James Madison, Sr., named it Montpelier.

Early Education

In 1762, James's father sent his son to a boarding school run by Donald Robertson. It was unusual for the boy to be sent away to school. Most wealthy Virginia planters hired their own tutors to teach their children. Robertson's school was located about seventy miles away from Montpelier. Two of James's cousins, James and Frances Taylor, already attended the school.

At Robertson's school, James studied mathematics, geography, and literature. He also studied Latin, Greek, Spanish, and French. Robertson loaned him books to read on philosophy and politics. The boy discovered he loved to learn, and he grew to greatly admire Robertson as a teacher. James left the school in September 1767, but he never forgot his years there. "All that I have been in life," he later wrote, "I owe largely to that man."[1]

At College in Princeton

At Montpelier, James's father had hired Thomas Martin, an Episcopalian minister, to teach his younger children. Martin lived with the family. Madison continued his studies with Martin as he prepared for college. In those days, young Virginians who attended college most often went to the College

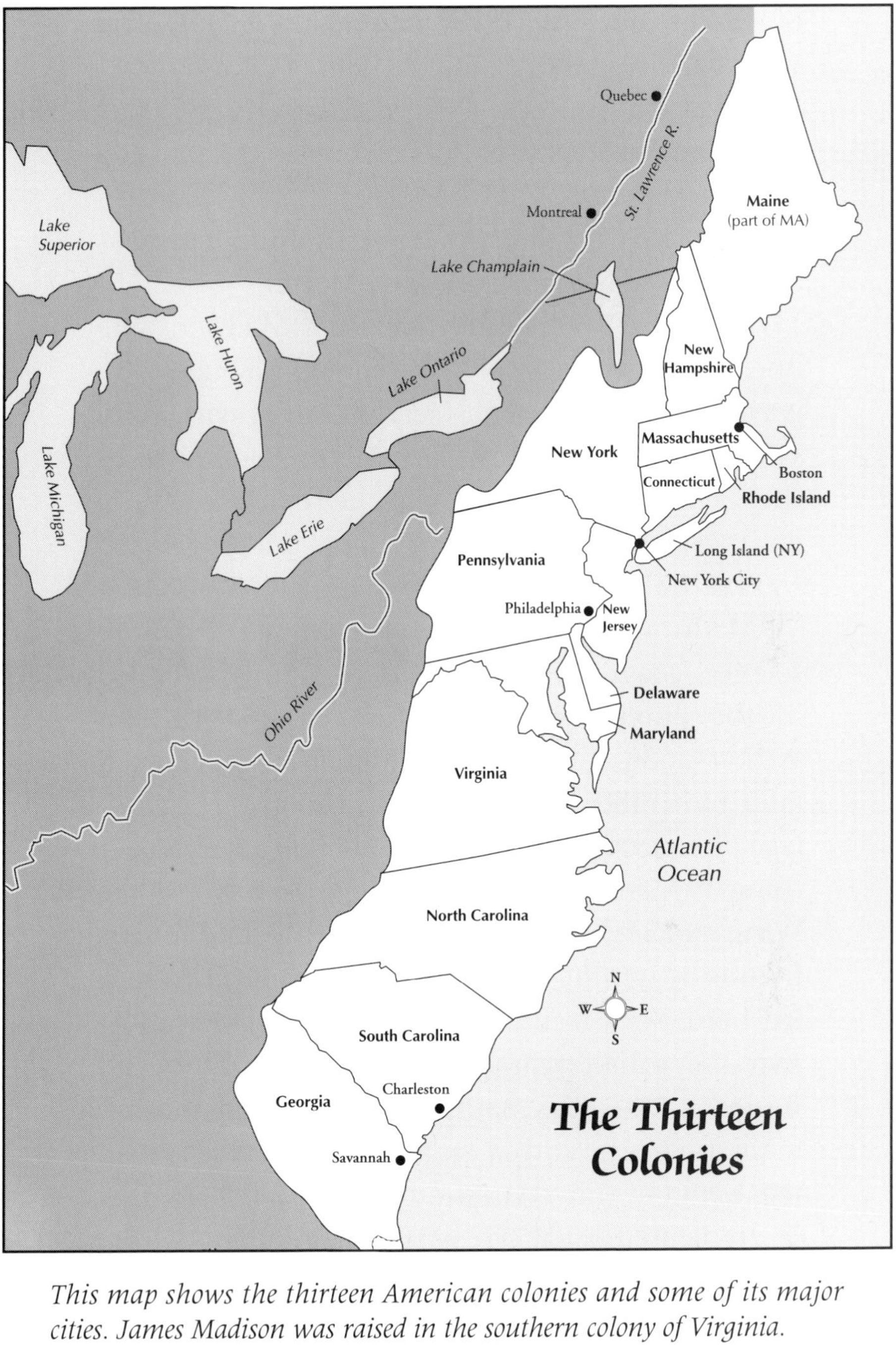

Quebec
St. Lawrence R.
Montreal
Maine
(part of MA)
Lake Superior
Lake Champlain
Lake Huron
New Hampshire
Lake Ontario
Lake Michigan
Massachusetts
New York
Boston
Connecticut
Rhode Island
Lake Erie
Long Island (NY)
Pennsylvania
New York City
Philadelphia
New Jersey
Ohio River
Delaware
Maryland
Virginia
Atlantic Ocean
North Carolina
N
W
E
S
South Carolina
Charleston
Georgia
Savannah
The Thirteen Colonies

This map shows the thirteen American colonies and some of its major cities. James Madison was raised in the southern colony of Virginia.

of William and Mary. It was located in Williamsburg, Virginia's colonial capital. Thomas Martin had attended the College of New Jersey (present-day Princeton University). Princeton was nearly 300 miles away. But James decided to follow Martin's example. He wanted to travel and study under teachers like those who had educated Martin.

In June 1769, eighteen-year-old Madison rode north on horseback. A slave named Sawney, who was Madison's personal servant, rode with him. When he reached Princeton, Madison enrolled in the College of New Jersey as a sophomore. The entire college was located in a large building called Nassau Hall.

Madison studied Latin, Greek, mathematics, science, geography, and philosophy. He also joined in the public debates encouraged by Dr. John Witherspoon, the college president. Witherspoon later remembered that while Madison was at college "he never knew him to do or say an improper thing."[2] Madison joined a college club called the Whig Society. He sometimes entertained his friends by writing comical poems. But he also studied hard. As a result, he earned his degree in just two and a half years. The constant study nearly ruined his health. Madison remembered that on many nights he stayed up late and slept "less than five hours in the twenty-four."[3]

In September 1771, Madison graduated from college along with eleven other classmates. For a time, he considered becoming a minister. He remained at Princeton another six months to study Hebrew and religion. He suffered from nervousness and poor health, though. He told one Princeton friend that he could not make plans for the future because he did not "expect a long or healthy life."[4]

Madison finally returned to Montpelier. Until 1775, he stayed there nursing his health. For a time, he considered becoming a lawyer. Thomas Martin had died. So in the meantime, Madison taught school to his siblings, Nelly, William, and Sarah.

"No Taxation without Representation!"

In the 1600s and 1700s, Great Britain established thirteen colonies along the Atlantic coast of North America. Great Britain's royal government appointed governors and other officials to rule the colonies. The colonists elected their own governing assemblies. But new laws, which the colonists were required to obey, were sometimes sent from Great Britain.

In 1765, American colonists protested a new British law called the Stamp Act. The Stamp Act taxed almost everything written or printed on paper. Pamphlets, newspapers, advertisements, deeds, and even playing cards were taxed. The British government had passed the Stamp Act to help pay the cost of the French and Indian War. That war, which occurred from 1754 to 1763, had been fought to protect the colonists. Therefore, the

British government believed the colonists should pay a large part of its cost.

Throughout the thirteen colonies, people were outraged by the Stamp Act. They did not want to pay the tax. The colonists were most upset because they had never been allowed to protest or vote in the British government. They had no elected representatives. To challenge the tax, many colonists chanted the slogan, "No Taxation without Representation!"

The British government did away with the Stamp Act in 1766. The following year, however, it passed new laws called the Townshend Acts. These laws taxed such items imported by the colonists as glass, paint, lead, cloth, wine, and tea. In Massachusetts, colonist Samuel Adams had organized a group of angry protesters called the Sons of Liberty. On the night of December 16, 1773, dozens of protesters disguised themselves as American Indians. They then boarded three cargo ships anchored in Boston Harbor. They dumped 342 chests of tea into the water. This protest became known as the Boston Tea Party.

The British government responded harshly to the Boston Tea Party. The next year, regiments of British soldiers landed in Boston. Massachusetts became occupied territory under military law. All the thirteen colonies now clearly understood the result of defying British laws.

Many Virginians supported the Massachusetts protests. Virginia sent delegates to the First Continental Congress in September 1774. The

Massachusetts citizens marched in protest of the Stamp Act. American colonists resented the fact that they had no voice in the British government.

Congress decided that the colonies should make a general protest by refusing to buy imported British goods. They would boycott all British trade. More and more Americans were feeling a desire to become independent from Great Britain. Madison himself grew very excited by the idea. In November 1774, he wrote that Virginians were filled with "a spirit of Liberty and Patriotism."[5]

The Orange County Committee of Safety

In December 1774, local voters elected twenty-three-year-old Madison to the Orange County

Committee of Safety. Madison's father was elected chairman. The duty of the Committee of Safety was to enforce the boycott. But it quickly became the local revolutionary government. Madison wrote in January 1775 that he expected to have thousands of well-trained men "ready to meet danger whenever it appears . . ."[6]

On April 21, 1775, British soldiers clashed with local militia in the towns of Lexington and Concord, Massachusetts. The bloody fight marked the beginning of the Revolutionary War. As war broke out, Madison and many of his friends joined the Orange County militia. Together, they practiced shooting muskets. In June 1775, he told a friend that he "should not often miss the bigness of a man's face at the distance of 100 Yards."[7] In the end, however, Madison's health kept him from marching off to war.

Madison continued to organize forces and collect supplies. In October 1775, the Virginia Committee of Safety appointed Madison "Colonel of the Militia of the County of Orange."[8] But this temporary force of volunteers was never asked to march off to battle.

The Virginia Convention

In April 1776, Orange County voters elected twenty-five-year-old Madison to represent them at the Virginia Convention. The Virginia Convention intended to establish a new, revolutionary government for Virginia. In May, Madison rode off to

Williamsburg. He joined Patrick Henry, George Mason, and other Virginia revolutionaries when he took his seat in the colonial House of Burgesses.

Madison immediately added his voice to those who demanded national independence from Great Britain. The convention delegates quickly prepared an independence resolution. They sent it to the Second Continental Congress meeting in Philadelphia. Virginia delegate Richard Henry Lee offered the independence resolution on June 7, 1776. The motion was accepted, and Thomas Jefferson wrote the Declaration of Independence soon after.

Massachusetts militiamen clashed with British soldiers on April 21, 1776. The Battles of Lexington and Concord marked the beginning of the Revolutionary War.

When the Declaration of Independence was adopted on July 4, 1776, the United States was born.

A New State Government

By that time, the Virginia Convention was already at work forming a new state government. Madison served on the committee that was preparing a state constitution and a declaration of rights. George Mason did most of the writing. But Madison made

In 1776, James Madison took his seat as a delegate to the Virginia Convention. The delegates gathered in the House of Burgesses in Virginia's colonial capitol of Williamsburg.

sure that freedom of religion was added.[9] As a result, the document included the promise that "all men are equally entitled to the free exercise of religion."[10]

The convention began debates on the state constitution on June 24. Every delegate voted in favor of it five days later. Madison never spoke publicly during the debates. But he did sometimes whisper his ideas to the men who sat near him. Fellow delegate Edmund Randolph quickly grew to admire Madison. Randolph later remarked that everyone who overheard Madison's whispered comments wanted "to sit daily within the reach of his conversation. . . ."[11] Madison's quiet but hard work at the convention caught the attention of Virginia's revolutionary leaders. He had clear ideas about democratic government. Randolph remembered, "Madison, even then, attracted great notice."[12]

The House of Delegates

In the fall of 1776, the Virginia Convention elected Patrick Henry first governor of the state. All the convention members, including Madison, automatically became members of the new House of Delegates. That fall, Madison met Thomas Jefferson for the first time. Jefferson recently had returned from the Second Continental Congress in Philadelphia.

Madison, at the age of twenty-five, stood five feet, six inches tall. He was slender with a boyish face and pale skin. Jefferson, on the other hand, was a tall, sturdy man of over six feet, two inches. Yet Madison discovered that he and Jefferson had much in common. Jefferson's Virginia home, Monticello, was only thirty miles southwest of Montpelier. The two men were both the sons of plantation owners. They also shared many of the same interests and political ideas. Madison found himself charmed by Jefferson's conversation.

Madison was defeated for reelection to the House of Delegates in April 1777. In Orange County, it was the custom for candidates to set up a large barrel of rum or hard cider on Election Day. Madison, however, refused to continue the custom. Giving away free drinks, Madison believed, was a shameful way for a candidate to win votes. Disappointed Orange County citizens voted against Madison and elected Charles Porter instead.[13]

Advisor to the Governor

In November 1777, the House of Delegates remembered Madison's talents. They elected him to a seat on the eight-member Council of State. These were the governor's close advisors. Madison began his new duties on January 14, 1778, and worked with Governor Patrick Henry.

In the middle of the Revolutionary War, there was plenty for the Virginia governor and his eight advisors to do. Soldiers and supplies were needed to send to General Washington's army. Beyond the Appalachian Mountains, forts were required to guard settlers against American Indian attacks. Ships had to be built to protect the Atlantic coast against British warships. The Virginia government needed to collect tax money to pay for everything. Henry also made special use of Madison's skill as a writer. Madison soon found himself penning all of the governor's official letters.

In the Continental Congress

In December 1779, Virginia's General Assembly chose Madison to be one of the state's delegates to the Continental Congress. Madison traveled by coach to Philadelphia over muddy roads. On March 18, 1780, he arrived with his personal servant, a slave named Billey. He took a room in a boarding house at Fifth and Market streets. It was located only a block from the Pennsylvania State House where Congress met.

Twenty-nine-year-old James Madison became the youngest man in the Congress. It was a gloomy time for the United States. The Revolutionary War already had been dragging on for five years. General Washington's ragged army was camped that winter at Morristown, New Jersey. The troops were in great need of food and supplies. But Congress seemed powerless to help. The government could not pay its bills or its soldiers. The day Madison arrived in Philadelphia, Congress voted on a new plan for raising money. It called upon the states to send larger contributions to the national treasury. Madison declared in a letter to Thomas Jefferson, who was serving as Virginia's governor at the time, "Believe me Sir as things now stand, if the States do not [provide money] we are undone."[14]

Mr. Madison

Madison soon took the lead in representing Virginia in Congress. "Mr. Madison . . . they say is clever in Congress," remarked Martha Bland, the wife of Virginia delegate Theodorick Bland. But she also thought him a "gloomy stiff creature."[15] However, Madison's quiet but steady work soon attracted attention.

One of Madison's concerns was the western territory beyond the Appalachian Mountains. This territory included all or parts of the present-day states of Ohio, Indiana, Illinois, Kentucky, Tennessee, Alabama, and Mississippi. Madison supported the idea that the region should be organized into separate states. He finally got his idea passed into law in 1783.

Madison took part in foreign matters, as well. In 1779, American diplomat Henry Laurens was captured by the British while sailing to Holland. He was thrown into prison in the Tower of London. Madison declared in Congress in December 1781 that "the dignity of the United States, as a sovereign and independent nation," required that American diplomats be treated with respect.[16]

Madison greatly believed that the Congress needed to be better informed. In January 1783, he proposed the establishment of a Library of Congress. His motion even included a list "of books proper for the use of Congress."[17] But at the time, Congress had no money to pay for such a library. The motion was voted down. Madison would have to wait until 1800 for Congress finally to create the Library of Congress.

A visiting Frenchman, the Chevalier de la Luzerne, described Madison as "the man of the soundest judgment in Congress."[18] Madison's reputation as a congressman was growing swiftly. During his first three years in Congress, however, Virginia failed to pay him. The state was not paying its proper share into the national treasury. His parents asked that he return home. But he answered that his public duties kept him in Philadelphia. Besides, he could not think of leaving without paying what he owed for room and board.

Unpaid Soldiers

George Washington won a stunning victory at Yorktown, Virginia, in October 1781. British Lord Charles Cornwallis surrendered his entire army of 7,000 men. The war and American independence were practically won. For the next two years, there was little fighting. With each passing month, however, American soldiers continued to demand their pay. But Congress had no money to give them.

On June 21, 1783, about three hundred angry enlisted soldiers marched into Philadelphia. They surrounded the State House, Madison recalled, "with the intent of not letting anyone leave."[19] Madison remembered how it looked and felt being trapped inside. "The soldiers remained in their position," he explained, "without offering any violence."[20] Some soldiers, however, shouted curses and pointed their muskets at the windows. At the end of the day, they finally allowed the congressmen to leave.

The threats of these unpaid soldiers scared the congressmen. They decided to conduct the government in a safer place. Madison found himself back in Princeton, New Jersey, where Congress gathered in September. His third one-year term would end in November. According to the Articles of Confederation, congressmen could not serve more than three years out of every six. As a result, Madison prepared to leave Congress. He had not been home in nearly four years.

Before leaving Congress, Madison's slave, Billey, ran away and then was recaptured. Madison wrote to his father, "I have judged it most prudent not to force Billey back to [Virginia]. . . . [I] cannot think of punishing him by transportation merely

In October 1781, Lord Cornwallis surrendered his army. American independence was almost won.

for coveting that liberty for which we have paid the price of so much blood, and have proclaimed so often to be the right . . . of every human being."[21] He arranged for Billey to earn his freedom working in Philadelphia. Madison's decision was not entirely an act of kindness. In Pennsylvania, Billey had seen what freedom was like. Madison feared what might happen if he brought his slave home. Billey might tell stories of freedom that would convince the other slaves to run away. Madison felt that the success of the Montpelier plantation depended upon slavery.

Elected to the House of Delegates

Madison returned home to Montpelier. In April 1784, however, Madison was again elected from Orange County to the Virginia House of Delegates. He journeyed to Richmond, the new state capital. Edmund Randolph wrote to Thomas Jefferson, "our friend of Orange will step . . . into the heat of battle."[22]

During three one-year terms in office, Madison helped write Virginia's laws. As chairman of the Committee on Commerce, Madison tried to make Norfolk, Virginia, a major ocean port. During 1784 and 1785, lawmakers led by Patrick Henry tried to get state aid for the Episcopal Church. Madison strongly spoke in favor of the separation of church and state. In the end, a majority of delegates agreed with him. They voted against Henry's plan.

The Annapolis Convention

In 1781, the Continental Congress had established a national government under a set of laws called the Articles of Confederation. The Articles of Confederation, however, were nothing more than a weak agreement between the states. The powers to tax, regulate trade between the states, and raise armies remained state powers.

In 1785, Congress decided that changes needed to be made. It asked the states to appoint delegates to meet in Annapolis, Maryland. The delegates were to design improved national trade laws. If the meeting failed, Madison commented, all the world would know "that we are not to be respected nor apprehended as a nation in matters of commerce."[23]

Madison was chosen a Virginia delegate to the Annapolis Convention. It met in September 1786. But only delegates from Virginia, Delaware, New Jersey, Pennsylvania, and New York attended. Nothing could be accomplished. Madison, Alexander Hamilton of New York, and other concerned delegates recommended that Congress call a second convention. Its purpose would be to revise the Articles of Confederation and make the national government stronger. Even George Washington approved the idea. "Thirteen sovereignties," Washington worried, "pulling against each other . . . will soon bring ruin on the whole."[24]

Designing a National Government

IN FEBRUARY 1787, Congress agreed that a convention should meet in Philadelphia in May to revise the Articles of Confederation. Twelve states agreed to send delegates. Only Rhode Island refused to take part.

Preparing for the Convention

Earlier, in November 1786, the Virginia Assembly had elected Madison to Congress. He had arrived in New York City, the temporary capital, in a snowstorm on February 9, 1787. "The present System," Madison declared in a letter, if not given some strong support, "will quickly tumble to the ground. No money is paid into the public Treasury; no respect is paid to the federal authority."[1] Madison understood the urgent need to change the present system of government.

Since 1785, Thomas Jefferson had been serving as United States minister to France. Madison had asked Jefferson to buy books for him while he was in Paris. The books Jefferson sent included encyclopedias and histories of Mexico, China, and European and ancient empires. Madison carefully studied these books. He did research to discover a solution for America. He became one of the world's leading experts on government. In the end, he decided that the Articles of Confederation could not be fixed. During the winter of 1786–1787, he wrote plans for what he thought would be the best form of government.

Arrival in Philadelphia

The Virginia Assembly voted to send seven delegates to Philadelphia to attend the Constitutional Convention. They included Edmund Randolph, George Washington, George Mason, George Wythe, John Blair, James McClurg, and James Madison. Madison reached Philadelphia on May 3, 1787. He arrived eleven days ahead of the convention's May 14 scheduled opening. But it was May 25 before enough delegates had arrived to begin.

At ten o'clock in the morning on May 25, the delegates entered the Pennsylvania State House (today's Independence Hall). In all, fifty-five delegates from twelve states would attend the convention. Among these were some of the most important men in America. They included George Washington, Alexander Hamilton, and Benjamin Franklin. Madison wrote to Jefferson: "The names of the members will satisfy you that the States have been serious in this business. . . . The whole Community is big with expectation. And there can be no doubt but that the result will in some way or other have a powerful effect on our destiny."[2]

The delegates immediately elected George Washington president of the Constitutional Convention. They also decided that their debates should remain secret. They even voted to move to the second floor of the State House. They wanted no one on the street outside to overhear what they were doing. They wished to debate without fear of outside influence or pressure. The Constitutional Convention met daily, six days a week, from late morning to early evening.

Madison had decided to keep a careful record of the convention debates. "I chose a seat," he later recalled, "in front of the presiding member, with the other members on my right and left hand. In this favorable position for hearing all that passed, I noted . . . what was read . . . or spoken. . . . I was not absent a single day, nor more than a casual fraction of an hour in any day, so that I could not have lost a single speech, unless a very short one."[3]

The Virginia Plan

On the morning of May 29, 1787, Virginia delegate Edmund Randolph stood and read to the

Constitutional Convention a prepared outline, which included fifteen steps for the creation of a new United States government, called the Virginia Plan. The Articles of Confederation were a failure, the outline declared. In their place, "a national Government ought to be established, consisting of a supreme Legislative, Executive and Judiciary."[4] Each of these three branches of government would have separate duties. The legislative branch (a Senate and a House of Representatives) would make laws. The executive branch (the president) would enforce the laws. The judicial branch (the court system) would interpret the laws. Each branch could prevent the other two from becoming too powerful. They could hold in check the actions of the others. It would be a system of checks and balances. James Madison had written most of the Virginia Plan, with some help from George Mason. With eight states present, the Constitutional Convention voted to design a new government based on the Virginia Plan.

Delegate Edmund Randolph introduced the Virginia Plan on May 29, 1787. It became the working model for the United States Constitution.

Early in June, Pennsylvania delegate James Wilson rose from his seat and addressed the Constitutional Convention. Wilson urged that a single president run the executive branch of the government. Benjamin Franklin argued, however, that there should be more than one president. Franklin feared that just one president would have too much power. He thought that a single president might too easily get the country into war. And who would run the country if one president fell ill? Most Americans wanted George Washington to be at the head of any new government. As leader of the Continental Army, Washington had proved his worth. In addition, James Wilson reminded the delegates that the people in the states were "accustomed and reconciled to a single executive."[5] In the end, the Constitutional Convention decided that a single president was the best idea for running the executive branch of government. On June 18, the convention voted to give the president veto power. By refusing to sign new laws, the president could prevent them from going into effect. At Madison's urging, however, the convention agreed that a two-thirds vote of Congress could overrule a presidential veto.

The structure of the legislative branch was not so easily decided. The Constitutional Convention agreed that it should consist of two chambers, a House of Representative and a Senate. The members of the Senate would be elected by the state legislatures. On June 6, Madison recorded in his notes that the delegates debated whether the House of Representatives should be elected

James Wilson was one of Madison's biggest allies in support of a strong national government.

by the people. Madison stood and insisted that the people must elect at least one branch of the legislature. The convention decided to discuss the issue later.

The New Jersey Plan

In a surprise move, on June 15, New Jersey delegate William Paterson rose and presented his New Jersey Plan. He offered it as a substitute for the Virginia Plan. Paterson and his supporters still believed that the Articles of Confederation could be repaired. The New Jersey Plan supported the idea of a one-chamber national legislature. Each state would get equal representation. It was the same governing method as in the Articles of Confederation.

On June 19, Madison stood and addressed the Constitutional Convention. He forcefully attacked the New Jersey Plan point by point. Madison declared that the New Jersey Plan wanted all the states to be "thrown into one mass and [divided] into 13 equal parts."[6] In answer to Madison's speech, the delegates voted to reject the New Jersey Plan. They would continue to use the Virginia Plan as their model.

Who Would Be Counted?

"[We are framing a system] which we wish to last for ages," Madison declared on June 26, 1787. The great problem continued to be how the House of Representatives should be structured. Connecticut delegates led by Roger Sherman submitted an idea on July 5. Their idea was that every state, big or small, would elect two senators. But members of the House of Representatives would be chosen based on state populations. Large states would have more members than small states. It would create a fair balance of power. "The Great Compromise" was passed on July 16.[7]

The delegates next had to decide how many representatives each state could send to the House. Many southern delegates insisted that slaves should be fully counted in state populations. Northern delegates did not like that idea. It would allow too many southerners in Congress. The Constitutional Convention finally settled on another compromise. Slaves would be counted as equal to three-fifths of a free white citizen. In addition, the southern states promised that no more slaves would be brought into the country after 1808.

If the delegates had not agreed on this issue, many angry southern delegates would have walked out of the Constitutional Convention. The three-fifths rule would remain part of the Constitution until the Thirteenth Amendment, which abolished slavery, was passed in 1865. The

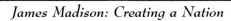

Fifteenth Amendment, passed in 1870, gave African-American men full voting rights.

Final Agreement

On July 26, 1787, the amended Virginia Plan was passed on to a Committee of Detail. Committee member James Wilson drew up a document that gave Congress seventeen basic powers. These began with the power to create and collect taxes followed by the power to regulate trade relations with foreign nations and the states. At the end of the list was the general power to "make all laws

---

Madison Stands Out

The Constitutional Convention remained at work from May until September 1787. During that time, Madison spoke 161 times. Only Gouverneur Morris of New York, who spoke 173 times, addressed the convention more often. South Carolina delegate Pierce Butler said of Madison, "Every person seems to acknowledge his greatness. . . . In the management of every great question he evidently took the lead in the Convention. . . ."[8]

Sometimes in debate, Madison became more excited than he wanted. He finally asked a friend to pull at his coattails if Madison seemed to show too much emotion. One day, after a long but brilliant speech, he said to his friend, "Why didn't you pull me when you heard me going on like that?" The friend responded, "I would rather have laid a finger on . . . lightning."[9]

---

which shall be necessary and proper" in order to carry on the government.[10]

The United States of America was to have a government containing executive, legislative, and judicial branches. The legislative branch would consist of a Senate and a House of Representatives. The Senate, with two members from each state, would be chosen by state legislatures for six-year terms. Members of the House of Representatives would be elected every two years by the people. The executive branch, the president, was to be chosen by electors. States could decide if their electors would be chosen by their legislatures or by popular votes. Each elector would cast a ballot with the names of two choices for president. The candidate with a majority of electoral votes would become president. The one with the second highest number would be named vice president. The president would have a four-year term, and could be reelected.

Madison failed to get everything he wanted in the planned new government. He had wanted members of the Senate to be chosen by popular election, the same way as in the House of Representatives. He had also wanted nine-year terms for senators. He had asked that the judicial branch (the court system) join the president in having veto power over laws passed by Congress. In addition, he had wanted Congress to have the power to overturn state laws.

Writing the Constitution

On September 8, 1787, a committee was chosen to prepare the final wording of the Constitution. The five men selected were Gouverneur Morris, William Samuel Johnson, Alexander Hamilton, Rufus King, and James Madison. They were called the Committee of Style and Arrangement.

It took them four days to finish their work. Gouverneur Morris did the actual writing. "The finish given to the style and arrangement of the Constitution," Madison wrote many years later,

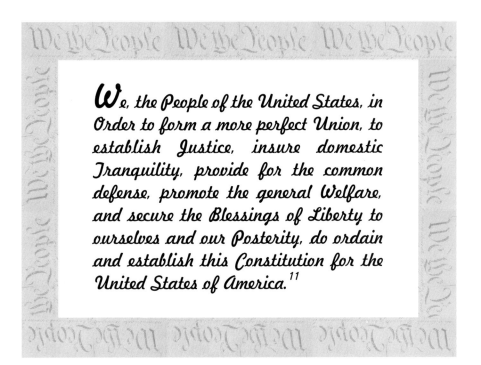

We, the People of the United States, in Order to form a more perfect Union, to establish Justice, insure domestic Tranquility, provide for the common defense, promote the general Welfare, and secure the Blessings of Liberty to ourselves and our Posterity, do ordain and establish this Constitution for the United States of America.[11]

Gouverneur Morris wrote the first sentences of the Constitution, the Preamble. They described the purpose of the document in stirring words.

"fairly belongs to the pen of Mr. Morris. . . . A better choice could not have been made."[12]

The Signing

Fifty-five delegates had attended the Constitutional Convention at one time or another. On September 17, 1787, thirty-eight remained in Philadelphia. Some delegates had been called home by their state governments. Others had walked out of the convention when things did not go their way.

On September 17, the Constitution was read aloud. Afterward, Benjamin Franklin rose with a speech in his hand. The old patriot did not have the energy to read it himself. James Wilson did that for him. "Mr. President," Franklin had written, "I confess that there are several parts of this constitution which I do not at present approve. . . ." But he added, "I consent, Sir, to this Constitution, because I expect no better and because I am not sure that it is not the best."[13] Madison's attitude was much the same as Franklin's. The Constitution did not include everything he wanted in a government. But he realized that it was the best government upon which the delegates could agree. In the end, the Constitution represented a national compromise of ideas.

The moment had arrived for the signing of the document. Each delegate stepped forward and dipped the pen in ink. Madison signed his name "James Madison, Jr." Three delegates, however,

The Rising Sun

While the last delegates were signing the Constitution, Benjamin Franklin pointed to the back of convention president George Washington's chair. Painted on it was half a sun poised over the horizon. Franklin remarked, "I have often and often in the course of the session . . . looked at [that sun] without being able to tell whether it was rising or setting: But now at length I have the happiness to know that it is a rising and not a setting sun."[14] His witty comment meant that he had hope for the country's future.

Benjamin Franklin

refused to sign: Elbridge Gerry of Massachusetts, Virginian George Mason, and Virginian Edmund Randolph. They believed that the new government would take too much power from the states. For Madison, though, it was a truly historic moment. His dream of a strong national government had become a reality.

United States Congressman

THE SIGNERS OF THE Constitution were amazed at what they had created. Washington declared that it was "much to be wondered at . . . little short of a miracle."[1] Just eight days after receiving the Constitution, Congress recommended that the states call conventions to ratify the document. "The Constitution," Madison wrote to Jefferson on December 9, 1787, "engrosses almost the whole political attention of America."[2]

There were Americans who angrily asked who had given these men the power to design a totally new government. In Virginia, Richard Henry Lee, George Mason, and Patrick Henry protested the Constitution. In Massachusetts, such old patriots as Samuel Adams and John Hancock also spoke out against it. "I have for some time been persuaded," Madison wrote to a Virginia friend in February 1788, "that the question on which the proposed Constitution must turn, is the simple one: whether the Union shall or shall not be continued."[3] Madison returned to the Confederation Congress in New York City. There, he wrote dozens of letters urging that the Constitution be ratified.

The Federalist

In October 1787, New Yorker Alexander Hamilton invited Madison to join him and John Jay in writing a series of newspaper articles. The articles would defend the Constitution. In general, Hamilton wrote about business issues. Jay, one of the nation's most experienced diplomats, wrote about United States international relations. Madison dealt with political ideas and compared the Constitution to other governments. Of the eighty-five articles published between October 1787 and March 1788, Hamilton wrote fifty-one, Madison twenty-nine, and Jay, who fell ill, five.

The articles first appeared in New York City newspapers. They were signed *Publius* (Latin for "the Public Man").[4] When a book of the collected essays was published in the spring of 1788, it was titled *The Federalist*.

The first article Madison wrote was No. 10 in the series. It appeared in *The Daily Advertiser* on November 23, 1787. In it, Madison explained the value of representative government. In No. 39, he explained, "We may define a republic to be . . . a government which derives all its powers directly or indirectly from . . . the people."[5] In No. 51, he stated, "It is of great importance in a republic . . . to guard one part of the society against the injustice of the other part."[6] "If men were angels," he reminded his readers, "no government would be necessary."[7]

People snatched up newspapers to read the articles. *The Federalist* won great support for the Constitution. Thomas Jefferson declared them "the best [review of] the principles of government which ever has been written."[8]

The First Congress of the United States

Delegates to the Virginia Convention gathered in June 1788. Patrick Henry tried to persuade Virginians to reject the Constitution. But Madison's careful arguments won the most support. On June 26, by a narrow margin, Virginia voted to ratify. In time, all thirteen states adopted the Constitution.

Patrick Henry remained a powerful politician in Virginia. Henry kept Madison from

In 1787, Alexander Hamilton invited Madison to join in writing articles defending the Constitution.

winning a seat in the new U.S. Senate. He also tried to keep Madison out of the House of Representatives. He persuaded James Monroe to challenge Madison for a seat in the first Congress. But Madison beat Monroe in his district by 336 votes in February 1789. During the campaign, Madison promised voters that he would offer amendments to the Constitution if elected. It was becoming clear that many people wanted certain freedoms to be guaranteed in the new government.

On the way to New York City, Madison stopped at George Washington's Virginia estate, Mount Vernon. Washington had been chosen by the Electoral College to be first President of the United States. Madison helped Washington prepare his inaugural address. Washington delivered it at Federal Hall in New York City on April 30, 1789, when he took the oath of office.

Madison quickly became a leader in the first session of Congress. On July 5, 1789, he wrote to his father:

> The business [of Congress] goes on ... very slowly. We are in a wilderness, without a single footstep to guide us. It is [therefore] necessary to explore the way with great labor and caution. Those who may follow will have an easier task.[9]

Massachusetts congressman Fisher Ames did not like Madison. "He speaks low," Ames commented, "his person is little and ordinary."[10] Yet even Ames had to admit that Madison was "devoted to public business, and a thorough master of almost every public question that can arise. . . . He will continue to be a very influential man in our country."[11]

Presidential Advisor

Although very busy in Congress, Madison spent many hours giving advice to President Washington. Washington believed that no one understood the Constitution better than Madison. Everything Washington did as president was being done for the first time. Madison advised Washington on how he should greet foreign ambassadors, address Congress, and meet with the public.

On May 19, 1789, Madison offered bills creating the Department of Foreign Affairs, the Treasury Department, and the War Department. Washington asked James Madison for advice on who should be offered positions in his cabinet. Alexander Hamilton became secretary of the treasury. Edmund Randolph became attorney general. Henry Knox was picked to be secretary of war. Madison was

President George Washington often called upon Madison for advice. In the new government, everything was being done for the first time and Washington wanted to perform his duties correctly.

especially helpful in persuading Thomas Jefferson to become secretary of state.

The Bill of Rights

At the Virginia Ratification Convention and during his election campaign, Madison had promised his support for a number of Constitutional amendments. These amendments would protect personal freedoms. On June 8, 1789, Madison offered a bill in Congress. It called for nineteen amendments. Madison stated, "It is my sincere opinion that the Constitution ought to be revised."[12]

Congress sent a number of Madison's suggestions to the states. They included freedom of religion, freedom of speech, the right to bear arms, and freedoms designed to protect citizens accused of crimes. By 1791, the states had ratified ten of the amendments known today as the Bill of Rights.

The Rise of Alexander Hamilton

Secretary of the Treasury Alexander Hamilton had always favored a strong national government. Hamilton was a lawyer and businessman. He supported the interests of the nation's merchants, bankers, and manufacturers. Jefferson and Madison, on the other hand, favored farmers. As time passed, Jefferson and Madison feared Hamilton's efforts to increase the federal government's powers. Hamilton wanted to interpret the Constitution more broadly than Madison had ever planned.

In the summer of 1789, Americans learned that a revolution had occurred in France. An extreme democratic government had been established. Hamilton distrusted the new French government. Instead, he favored better relations with Great Britain. Jefferson and Madison, however, believed that the French Revolution would become another great leap for democracy, like the American Revolution. Hamilton's political supporters began calling themselves Federalists. Jefferson's supporters took the name Republicans. (Jefferson's Republicans, in time, came to be called the Democratic-Republican Party and today are known more simply as the Democratic Party.) Madison, as Jefferson's supporter, led the Republicans in Congress.

Through the winter of 1789, Congress battled over where to locate the permanent national capital. New Englanders preferred New York City. Pennsylvanians desired Philadelphia. Virginians wanted a new capital to be built in the South, on the Maryland side of the Potomac River. Federalist congressmen finally struck a bargain with Republican congressmen. In exchange for a national banking system and other nationalist programs, the Federalists agreed to support the plan for a Potomac capital. Congress voted that Philadelphia be the temporary capital until 1800. Then the government would move south to the newly created federal District of Columbia.

Falling Out of Favor

As time passed, President Washington decided to support many of Hamilton's Federalist ideas. Philip Freneau, Madison's Princeton classmate, founded the *National Gazette*, and Madison contributed articles that often criticized Washington's policies. After February 1790, Washington relied on Madison's advice much less.

In 1793, war broke out between France and Great Britain. On April 22, Washington issued a Proclamation of Neutrality. He refused to let the United States become an ally of France. The United States would remain neutral, uncommitted. Madison, who strongly supported France, disagreed with this position. His relationship with Washington grew even more strained.

Dolley Payne Todd

During the summer of 1793, yellow fever spread throughout Philadelphia. Mosquitoes carried the deadly disease, although people did not realize it. Altogether, 5,000 people in the city died. Among the victims was a Quaker lawyer named John Todd. Todd's death left his young wife, Dolley Payne Todd, a widow.

Dolley had been born on May 29, 1768. She grew up on a plantation in Goochland County, Virginia. While still a child, her father, John Payne, joined the Quaker religion. The Quakers did not believe in slavery. In 1782, Payne freed his slaves and sold his Virginia plantation. He moved his family north to Philadelphia. There, he started a starch factory. (Starch is a powder that laundries use to stiffen shirt collars and cuffs.) But John Payne's company failed in 1789. He could not pay his debts. According to the Quaker faith, a good Quaker was free of all debts. The Quakers soon expelled Payne from the church. Deeply ashamed, Payne stayed in his bedroom until he died. To support the family, his wife turned their home into a boarding house.

Dolley grew into an attractive, lively woman. In 1790, she married John Todd. The couple had two sons by August 1793, when yellow fever broke out. Dolley and her two-year-old son, Payne, survived the fever. But John Todd and the youngest child died. She became a widow at the age of twenty-five.

Dolley attracted notice when she went out walking in Philadelphia. Many members of Congress grew to admire her. In May 1794, Madison asked New York Senator Aaron Burr to introduce him to Dolley. Burr knew Dolley because he had roomed in her mother's boarding house. Dolley wrote excitedly to her cousin Eliza Collins, "Thou must come to me. Aaron Burr says that the great little Madison has asked to be brought to see me this evening."[13]

After a swift romance, forty-three-year-old Madison and twenty-six-year-old Dolley Payne Todd were married on September 15, 1794. They married at Harewood in present-day Jefferson County, West Virginia. Harewood was the estate of Dolley's sister and her husband. Dolley had written to her cousin

Eliza, "In the course of this day I give my hand to the man of all others I most admire."[14]

Out of Public Office

Washington refused to run for a third four-year term in 1796. In the election race that year, the Electoral College chose Vice President John Adams to become second President of the United States. Thomas Jefferson received the second highest number of votes. As a result, he became vice president.

In the summer of 1797, Madison returned home to Montpelier. He had refused to run for another term in Congress. He wanted to take a rest from

In 1794, James Madison and Dolley Payne Todd were married at the estate of Harewood.

politics. His brother, Ambrose, had died in 1793. His father was growing old and was in bad health. Madison actively began to run the family plantation. He also started plans to remodel Montpelier. Thomas Jefferson had an ironworks at Monticello. Madison purchased 100,000 nails from his friend. He also ordered 190 windowpanes from France.

France's war with Great Britain continued to rage in 1797. American merchant ships traded with both nations. Sometimes French warships seized American ships bound for Great Britain. President John Adams sent diplomats to France to discuss the tense situation. The American diplomats soon reported that French foreign minister Charles Maurice de Talleyrand had demanded a bribe before he would agree to meet with them. Talleyrand's secret agents, who had made the demand, were referred to as X, Y, and Z.

News of the XYZ Affair outraged most Americans. Many people demanded war with France. In 1798, Congress ordered military preparations. As war fever gripped the nation, Congress also passed several laws known as the Alien and Sedition Acts. They were to stay in effect for two years. The Alien Act extended the residence requirement for American citizenship from five to fourteen years. The Sedition Act gave the president the power to arrest or deport dangerous foreigners during wartime. The Sedition Act called for fines and prison terms for anyone who wrote or spoke out against the government. Fines could be as high as five thousand dollars and prison terms as long as five years. The Sedition Act suddenly made it illegal to speak freely.

The Alien and Sedition Acts clearly contradicted the First Amendment to the Constitution. But President Adams still signed them into law. "The Alien bill . . . is a monster," declared Madison, "that must for ever disgrace its parents."[15] Thomas Jefferson responded to the Alien and Sedition Acts by writing his Kentucky Resolutions. Presented to the Kentucky legislature, they declared the Alien and Sedition Acts unconstitutional. Jefferson believed that states had the right to completely overturn laws they thought were unconstitutional. He urged Madison to write similar resolutions to be offered to the Virginia Assembly. Madison took up his pen. Madison's Virginia Resolutions were less extreme than Jefferson's Kentucky Resolutions. Madison urged the Virginia legislature to demand that Congress rescind the Alien and Sedition Acts. But he suggested that the court system should decide if laws were constitutional. "The genius of the Constitution," wrote Madison, "and the opinion of the people of the United States, cannot be overruled by those who administer the Government."[16]

In the fall of 1798, however, both Kentucky and Virginia failed to act on Jefferson's and Madison's resolutions. Fortunately, the United States and France eventually agreed to renew peaceful relations. The Alien and Sedition Acts were allowed to expire after two years.

Secretary of State

IN THE ELECTION of 1800, John Adams was defeated in his campaign for a second term as president. When the electors' ballots were counted, however, a tie for first place was discovered. Thomas Jefferson and his running mate, Aaron Burr, each received 73 votes. The tense deadlock was finally broken by a vote in the House of Representatives. It was decided Thomas Jefferson would become third President of the United States and Aaron Burr vice president.

The Department of State

On March 4, 1801, Jefferson asked forty-nine-year-old Madison to become secretary of state. On May 2, he took the oath of office as secretary of state.

In 1801, Washington, D.C., was still a town of only three thousand people. Stonemasons were just finishing construction on a number of government buildings. The State Department and the War Department shared a new building, near the President's Mansion on Pennsylvania Avenue. At the time, the entire staff of the State Department consisted of just eight clerks and a messenger.

The State Department had a number of important duties. It contained the patent office, where new inventions were registered. It also contained the bureau of the census, where population records were kept. The government's printing presses were operated at the State Department. The presses printed copies of new laws and other government documents for the public.

Madison quickly realized that foreign affairs would take up most of his time. He had never traveled outside the United States. But he would do his best to handle America's relations with foreign countries.

The Louisiana Purchase

In 1803, Jefferson and Madison appointed James Monroe as a special diplomat to go to Europe. Monroe was to join U.S. Minister Robert Livingston in France. The two diplomats were ordered to buy the city of New Orleans, Louisiana, and the territory of Florida for the United States. New Orleans was part of the Louisiana Territory, which was controlled by France. Florida was owned by Spain.

At this time, Napoleon Bonaparte, First Consul of France, realized that he needed money to fight his wars in Europe. In April 1803, Napoleon offered to sell the entire Louisiana Territory to the United States. It included all of present-day Arkansas, Iowa, Missouri, and Nebraska, as well as parts of Louisiana, Minnesota, Oklahoma, Kansas, Colorado, Wyoming, Montana, North Dakota, and South Dakota.

Secretary of State Madison was amazed when he learned of Napoleon's offer. Monroe and Livingston soon arranged to pay $15 million for the Louisiana Territory. Madison received the treaty on July 14, and Congress quickly agreed to it. The Louisiana Territory was officially turned over to the United States on December 20, 1803. Overnight, the country had doubled in size. American settlers, eager for land, soon began pouring across the Mississippi River. Madison was greatly pleased that America had made the

In April 1803, Napoleon Bonaparte surprised Madison by offering to sell the entire Louisiana Territory to the United States.

Louisiana Purchase. The growth of the United States would surely make it a great nation.[1]

American Manners

A new British minister, Anthony Merry, arrived in Washington, D.C., in the fall of 1803. Secretary of State Madison took Merry to be officially presented to President Jefferson. Merry was shocked to see how Jefferson greeted him. Jefferson had not bothered to dress up for the meeting. Merry later stated that Jefferson was "not merely in undress, but actually standing in slippers [worn] down at the heels."[2] Merry complained to Madison about this insult. But Madison calmly explained that the minister from Denmark had been welcomed the same way.

On December 2, Jefferson entertained the Merrys at an official dinner at the President's Mansion. Jefferson's wife had died, so Dolley Madison usually served as his official hostess. When dinner was announced, Jefferson offered to escort Dolley Madison to the table. He ignored her whisper, "Take Mrs. Merry."[3] The Merrys had to find seats for themselves among the general rush of guests. "This will be cause of war," whispered the wife of the Spanish minister.[4] Merry was outraged by Jefferson's apparent lack of manners. As an important diplomat, he expected better treatment. He soon reported to his government, "Everything else in the federal city is equally as perfectly savage."[5]

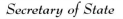
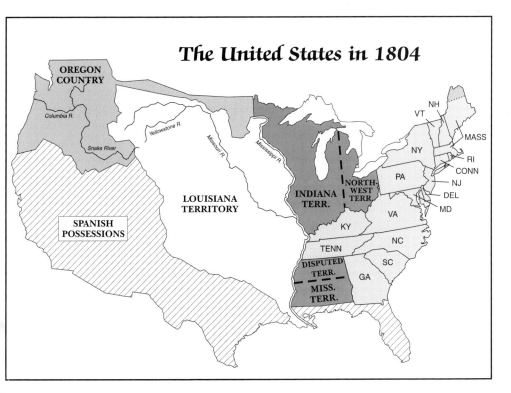

This map shows the United States after the Louisiana Purchase.

Madison approved of these new American manners. Jefferson was determined to treat everyone equally. No one got special attention from him. Madison had earlier stated, "The more simple, the more republican we are in our manners, the more national dignity we shall acquire."[6]

The *Leopard* and the *Chesapeake*

Great Britain and France were again at war in 1807. On January 7, the British government declared that American ships could be seized if

In his dress, he. . . . always appeared neat . . . in the costume of a well-bred . . . old school gentlemen. I have heard in early life he sometimes wore light-colored clothes. But . . . I never knew him to wear any other color than black. . . . In height he was about five feet six inches, of small and delicate form. . . . his hair was originally of a dark brown color; his eyes were bluish; his form, features, and manner were not commanding, but . . . few men possessed so rich a flow of language, or so great a fund of amusing anecdotes, which were made the more interesting from their being well-timed and well-told.[7]

Edward Coles served as Madison's private secretary for six years. He left this description of Madison.

they attempted to trade with France. The British also claimed the right to seize sailors on American ships. They claimed that they had the right to force them, or impress them, into the British Navy. The United States, Madison responded, "can never acknowledge any other nation to take from their vessels on the high sea any persons whatever."[8] Madison told British Minister Merry, "The American flag should give complete protection to whatever persons might be under it."[9]

On June 22, 1807, the British warship *Leopard* sighted the American warship *Chesapeake* on the Atlantic coast just off Norfolk, Virginia. The captain of the *Leopard* demanded the return of British sailors he claimed were on board the *Chesapeake*. When Captain James Barron refused, the *Leopard* suddenly fired its cannons. The *Chesapeake* was not prepared for the attack and suffered heavy damage. Smashed masts crashed down onto the deck. Water poured in through twenty-two holes in its hull. Three Americans were killed and eighteen wounded. Finally, Captain Barron surrendered his ship. The British boarded and seized four sailors. Madison was

Thomas Jefferson believed manners should be informal in a democratic nation. The way that Jefferson dressed and received guests upset some British diplomats in Washington, D.C.

greatly angered when he learned this news. Great Britain, he declared, "would be second to none in resenting . . . such an insult to her flag."[10]

The Embargo Act

The British government refused to apologize for its attack on the *Chesapeake*. Across the country, Americans talked of war. Madison had his own idea of how the nation should react. He suggested that the United States cut off trade with Great Britain. He believed that Great Britain would stop impressing sailors if threatened with the loss of such American goods as food, tobacco, and lumber.

On December 18, 1807, President Jefferson asked for an embargo. The law would stop all of America's international trade. "The people of this Country will bear with cheerfulness any sacrifices . . . which these embargo laws will impose upon them," declared the Richmond *Enquirer*.[11] But the Embargo Act did not work as Jefferson and Madison had hoped. Great Britain seemed unaffected by the loss of American trade. However, New England's harbors were soon filled with idle ships and unemployed sailors. The economy of New England crashed. On March 1, 1809, the failed embargo was ended.

Improvements at Montpelier

Remodeling work at Montpelier continued throughout this period. British diplomat Augustus Foster visited Montpelier in 1807. Foster noticed that the plantation was able to support itself completely. He explained in a letter home:

> When at a distance from any town, it is necessary they should be able to do all kinds of handiwork; and accordingly, at Montpelier, I found a forge, a turner's shop, a carpenter, and wheelwright. All articles that were wanted for farming or the use of the house were made on the spot, and I saw a very well-constructed waggon that had just been completed.[12]

The Election of 1808

At the end of his two terms, Thomas Jefferson thought that Madison should follow him into office. Republicans in Congress nominated Madison for president in the spring of 1808. Troubles with Great Britain still darkly loomed. The *National Intelligencer* called Madison the man "best fitted to guide us through the impending storm."[13]

The Federalists selected Charles Cotesworth Pinckney of South Carolina as their choice for president. Through the campaign, Madison remained at Montpelier. Back then, it was considered good manners for a presidential candidate to simply wait and be chosen for office. One friend later wrote, "While a candidate for the presidency, no one . . . ever heard him open his lips or say one word on the subject."[14]

In the fall, the seventeen states chose their presidential electors. On December 7, the electors finally cast their votes. The results were revealed: Madison 122, Pinckney 47, and New York Governor

George Clinton 6. James Madison easily had been elected fourth President of the United States. Americans had decided that Madison could defend the nation. Secretary of the Treasury Albert Gallatin remarked, "Mr. Madison is, as I always knew him, slow in taking his ground, but firm when the storm arises."[15]

The Fourth President

IN WASHINGTON, D.C., cannons boomed in celebration on Inauguration Day, March 4, 1809. Thousands of people crowded around the Capitol and along Pennsylvania Avenue. At noon, fifty-seven-year-old James Madison rode in a carriage escorted by a troop of cavalry to the Capitol. He entered the crowded House of Representatives, where a committee of senators led him to the front of the chamber.

Before taking the oath of office, Madison delivered his inaugural address. "Mr. Madison was extremely pale and trembled excessively when he first began to speak," noticed one witness, "but soon gained confidence and spoke audibly."[1] In his speech, Madison stated, "The present situation of the world is indeed without a parallel and that of our own country full of difficulties."[2]

A Day of Celebrations

Madison was sworn in by Chief Justice John Marshall. Afterward, the new president returned to his home on F Street, where he held an open house. Margaret Bayard Smith, wife of the editor of the *National Intelligencer*, wrote in a letter, "Today after the inauguration, we all went to Mrs. Madison's. The street was full of carriages and people, and we had to wait near half an hour, before we could get in,—the house was completely filled. . . . Near the door of the drawing room Mr. and Mrs. Madison stood to receive their company."[3]

In the evening, an inaugural ball was held at Long's Hotel. Margaret Bayard Smith, who attended, was greatly impressed with Dolley Madison. "She looked a queen," Smith recorded. "She had on a pale buff colored velvet [gown] beautiful pearl necklace, earrings and bracelets. Her head dress was a turban of . . . velvet and white satin. . . ."[4] Dolley Madison greatly enjoyed entertaining. But the day's excitement had tired her husband. President Madison remarked to Smith, "I would much rather be in bed."[5]

Forming a Cabinet

Madison chose William Eustis of Massachusetts to become secretary of war. He picked Paul Hamilton of South Carolina for secretary of the navy. Caesar Rodney of Delaware remained for a time as attorney general.

Most importantly, Madison wanted to shift Jefferson's secretary of the treasury, Albert Gallatin, to the position of secretary of state. But Gallatin had political enemies. Maryland Senator Samuel Smith vowed that he would block Gallatin's nomination. In order to keep Gallatin at the Treasury Department at least, Madison promised to name Smith's brother, Robert, as secretary of state. Unfortunately, Robert Smith had little skill as a diplomat. As a result, Madison found himself still handling the most important duties of the State Department.

Dolley Madison in the White House

In 1809, the President's Mansion was just beginning to be called the "White House." Dolley Madison spent her first months in the White House buying new furniture. Congress provided $26,000 for this purpose, a huge sum at the time. Dolley hired architect Benjamin Henry Latrobe to do the decorating. Latrobe spent $2,150 just on three expensive mirrors. He paid another $458 for a piano Dolley wanted.

On May 31, 1809, Dolley Madison held her first Wednesday evening levee at the White House. A levee was a public gathering where everyone was welcome to meet the president. James and Dolley Madison, remarked one British guest, seemed very different. She was always cheerful, while Madison

Dolley Madison loved entertaining guests at the White House.

was "a very small thin pale-visaged man of rather a sour, reserved and forbidding countenance."[6]

Dolley often wore jeweled and feathered turbans. She was easy to recognize. She also used rouge and lipstick, which was something new in America at the time. James Madison usually dressed in black. But his wife always wore the latest colorful fashions from Paris. She seemed the perfect hostess, full of warmth and charm. She also had an excellent memory and could remember peoples' names and faces.

Relations With Great Britain

Relations between the United States and Great Britain were growing worse. British warships continued to stop American merchant ships and impress sailors. Great Britain still refused to apologize for the attack on the *Chesapeake*. In March 1809, Congress passed a new law. It cut off trade with the warring nations of Great Britain and France. Madison put his faith in this second embargo act.

In April, British Minister David Erskine suddenly told Madison of his country's desire for normal trade relations. Erskine even hinted that Great Britain would apologize for the attack on the *Chesapeake*. Madison left Washington, D.C., on July 20, full of hope for a peaceful future. He spent the summer at Montpelier, where two one-story wings were being added to the mansion.

Madison was at Montpelier when he learned that the British government refused to honor Erskine's offers. In fact, Erskine was ordered to sail home to Great Britain in disgrace. When Madison returned to Washington, D.C., he suggested that Congress begin spending more money building forts and warships. The nation should prepare itself in case there should be war.

Presidential Decisions

Although it was controlled by Spain, West Florida was mostly settled by Americans. It was the part of Florida that included the coastal regions of present-day Mississippi and Alabama. The United States had first claimed the territory in 1803. On October 27, 1810, Madison ordered soldiers into West Florida. He had decided to take definite possession of the region. Governor William Claiborne of the Orleans Territory soon established American control there.

The War Hawks

In the fall elections of 1810, sixty-three new members won seats in the House of Representatives.

Most of these new congressmen were Republicans. They included such men as Henry Clay, Richard M. Johnson, Felix Grundy, and John C. Calhoun. Many of these new congressmen loudly called for war with Great Britain. They demanded that America's neutral rights at sea be respected. But they also wanted war to conquer the British territory of Canada and add it to the United States. As a group, these congressmen soon became known as the War Hawks. The War Hawks proudly made "Free Trade and Sailors' Rights" their rally cry.[7]

Feuding in his cabinet kept Madison busy in March 1811. Albert Gallatin threatened to resign as secretary of the treasury. But Madison could not afford to lose such a valued cabinet member. Instead, he fired Gallatin's enemy, Robert Smith. He named James Monroe as the new secretary of state. Louis Serurier, the French minister to the United States, commented, "Mr. Madison [is] not without some toughness of character."[8]

In July, Madison left Washington, D.C., for another summer vacation at Montpelier. The new one-story wings were finally finished. The family mansion now stretched 150 feet from end to end. "We passed two months on our mountain in health and peace, " wrote Dolley Madison.[9]

That fall, American Indians in the Indiana Territory rose up and threatened war. Many Americans insisted that the British were giving support to the Shawnee leader Tecumseh. General

William Henry Harrison marched an army into the region to protect western settlers. On November 7, 1811, Harrison battled Shawnees led by Tecumseh's brother, the Prophet. Harrison's success near the Tippecanoe River won him the nickname "Old Tippecanoe."

"I believe there will be war," Dolley Madison wrote to her sister on December 20, 1811. "Mr. Madison sees no end to [our problems] without it."[10] The British had impressed 6,257 sailors from American ships since 1803.

In 1811, Henry Clay was one of the many new congressmen who demanded war with Great Britain. This group came to be known as the War Hawks.

On January 11, 1812, Congress voted to raise 35,000 more soldiers to defend American territory. Madison still hoped for peace. But a Washington newspaper declared in May, "The final step ought to be taken, and that step is WAR."[11]

A Declaration of War

On May 13, 1812, a committee of War Hawk congressmen visited Madison at the White House. They promised that Congress would vote for war if he asked. Madison finally made his decision. On June 1, 1812, he sent a war message to the House of Representatives. To Congress, he listed "the . . . injuries and [insults] which have been heaped on our country. . . ."[12] In his message, Madison declared that Great Britain, "by the conduct of her government, presents a series of acts, hostile to the United States. . . ."[13] On June 4, the House of Representatives voted for war, 79 to 49. On June 17, the Senate also voted for war, 19 to 13. The next day, Madison signed the war declaration.

By a twist of fate, also on June 17, the British government ordered an end to impressments. The

"Tippecanoe and Tyler, Too"

After the War of 1812, William Henry Harrison served as a senator in Congress. He was also appointed U.S. minister to Colombia in 1828. Politicians chose Harrison as their candidate for president in 1840. They picked Senator John Tyler of Virginia to run for vice president. During the campaign, Harrison supporters reminded voters that Harrison, "Old Tippecanoe," had been a war hero. "Tippecanoe and Tyler, Too," they chanted at rallies and wrote on banners. In the fall election, Harrison beat Democratic candidate Martin Van Buren. But Harrison served the shortest time in office of any American president. He caught a cold on Inauguration Day, March 4, 1841, and died of pneumonia just one month later on April 4.

William Henry Harrison

British cruisers have been in the continued practice of violating the American flag . . . and of seizing and carrying off persons sailing under it . . . thousands of American Citizens, under the safeguard of public law, and of their national flag, have been torn from their country, and from everything dear to them, have been dragged on board ships of war of a foreign nation. . . .[14]

Madison's war message talked about the issue of impressment.

War of 1812 began one day after its main cause disappeared. But news traveled slowly in the days before the telegraph. Ships carried mail across the Atlantic and an ocean crossing took a month to six weeks. The British news arrived too late to keep America from plunging into war.

Mr. Madison's War

FEDERALISTS IN NEW ENGLAND were against the war. They quickly labeled it "Mr. Madison's War."[1] Supporters of the war called it "The Second War of American Independence."[2] In 1812, the United States was totally unprepared to fight. At the War Department, Secretary of War William Eustis only employed eight clerks. There were no more than 7,000 regular soldiers serving in the entire army. President Madison showed his concern. Attorney General Richard Rush would later recall, "He visited in person—a thing never known before—all the offices of the departments of war and navy, [ordering action] in a manner worthy of a . . . commander-in-chief."[3]

The Surrender of Detroit

In 1812, the Michigan Territory was still a frontier wilderness. Brigadier General William Hull, with 2,000 volunteer soldiers, occupied Fort Detroit. Madison ordered Hull to attack Fort Malden in Ontario, Canada. Hull did cross the Detroit River, but withdrew again before attacking the fort. British General Isaac Brock boldly crossed his small army into Michigan and soon surrounded Fort Detroit. In a panic, on August 16, Hull surrendered the fort and his entire army without firing a shot.

Madison was shocked to learn of the surrender. From Montpelier, he sent hurried letters to members of his cabinet. It was decided that Fort Detroit must be retaken. Generals James Winchester and William Henry Harrison were ordered to begin the long march into Michigan with 2,000 troops.

Brave Sailors

Surprisingly, America's first victories in the war were battles at sea. At the time, there were no more than seventeen warships in the U.S. Navy. Great Britain had a huge navy of about seven hundred warships.

Captain Isaac Hull commanded the U.S.S. *Constitution*. On August 19, 1812, Hull attacked the British warship *Guerrière* in the Atlantic Ocean. "Now boys," Hull exclaimed to his gunners, "pour it into them."[4] The *Constitution*'s roaring cannons sent cannonballs smashing into the *Guerrière*'s hull and ripping through its sails. In less than half an hour, the *Guerrière* was forced to surrender. Its hull

The United States warship Constitution *battled the British* Guerrière *on August 19, 1812. The* Constitution*'s strong hull won it the nickname "Old Ironsides."*

was so badly damaged, the ship soon sank beneath the waves. It was in this historic battle that the *Constitution*'s sturdy hull earned it the nickname "Old Ironsides."[5] During the fight, an American sailor had noticed a British cannonball bounce off the *Constitution*'s side.

The *Constitution*'s thrilling victory was soon followed by others. The American warship *Wasp* defeated the British warship *Frolic* on October 17. On October 25, Captain Stephen Decatur in command of the *United States* captured the British *Macedonian*. In December, the *Constitution*, now under the command of Captain William Bainbridge, destroyed the British warship *Java*. Americans lit bonfires and cheered in the streets at the news of these successes at sea. The giant British Navy was being stung by America's little fleet.

The Election of 1812

In the fall elections of 1812, Republicans campaigned for Madison's election to a second term as president. "The mild Mr. Madison is as determined and straight-forward a statesman as any country can boast," declared one Philadelphia newspaper.[6]

This cartoon shows Brother Jonathan, a symbol of the United States, giving a bloody nose to King George III. During the War of 1812, American victories at sea were showing the world that the United States would not be bullied by Great Britain.

Vice President George Clinton had died on April 20. Republicans chose Elbridge Gerry to be Madison's vice presidential running mate.

Not all Republicans were in favor of Madison. New York Republicans put forward New York City mayor DeWitt Clinton for president. The Federalists could not settle on a candidate of their own. They decided to support Clinton, with Philadelphia lawyer Jared Ingersoll running for vice president.

Clinton's campaign was not an honest one. Clinton campaigners in New England, where the war was unpopular, demanded that the fighting end. "Madison and War! or Clinton and Peace," chanted Clinton supporters.[7] But outside New England, Clinton's supporters made speeches in favor of the war.

Throughout the campaign, Madison remained silent. Many Americans still supported the war. The success of the navy certainly boosted hopes. In the West, settlers wanted revenge for Hull's shameful loss of Fort Detroit. When the electors of the eighteen states finally cast their ballots, the vote revealed: Madison 128, Clinton 89. Madison had won a second term as president.

Reorganizing the Cabinet

In December 1812, Madison decided to reorganize his cabinet. It was clear that he needed to make some changes. Secretary of the Navy Paul Hamilton was an alcoholic and unfit for office. To

Gerrymandering

Elbridge Gerry was a creative Republican politician. By national law, every ten years the states were required to redesign congressional district boundaries according to the population count. While governor of Massachusetts in 1812, Gerry approved designs that made sure plenty of Republican voters were living within each district. One strangely shaped new district had boundaries that made it look something like a salamander. As a result, Benjamin Russell, editor of the Boston *Centinel*, jokingly called it a "gerrymander."[8] Today, this method of obtaining seats in Congress is still called gerrymandering.

Elbridge Gerry

replace him, Madison chose William Jones of Pennsylvania.

Madison also decided that William Eustis was not doing a good job as secretary of war. He replaced Eustis with John Armstrong of New York. Congressman Jonathan Roberts praised the president's decisions: "Madison has now formed a cabinet that will conduct us to peace if any human means can do it."[9]

"Don't Give Up the Ship!"

In his 1813 inaugural address, Madison declared, "Already have the gallant exploits of our naval heroes proved to the world our inherent capacity to maintain our rights on one element."[10]

Not every sea battle, however, ended with American victory. In June 1813, Captain James Lawrence made the mistake of sailing out to sea with an untrained crew. Off the coast of Massachusetts, his ship, the *Chesapeake*, was attacked by the British warship *Shannon*. The *Chesapeake* was forced to surrender. In the fight, Lawrence had fallen with a deadly wound. His last words, "Don't give up the ship," instantly became an American war cry.[11]

In the hope of ending the war, President Madison decided to create a peace commission. John Quincy Adams, who was U.S. minister to Russia, headed it. It also included Albert Gallatin and James Bayard, who sailed for Europe on May 9, 1813. Payne Todd was also aboard the ship. Madison's twenty-one-year-old stepson would serve the Americans as a secretary. Later, Madison added Henry Clay and Jonathan Russell to the peace commission. They would meet with British officials in the city of Ghent (in present-day Belgium).

The Battle of Lake Erie

Through the summer of 1813, Captain Oliver Hazard Perry had been constructing an American navy on Lake Erie. In September, his nine ships at last set sail. Perry's flagship was named the *Lawrence* in honor of Captain Lawrence. The words,

"Don't give up the ship," were written on the ship's large, blue flag.

On September 10, Perry's squadron battled six British ships at close range. The *Lawrence* soon began to sink. With most of his crew dead or wounded, Perry entered a rowboat. He was rowed across the water to the American ship *Niagara*. Aboard the *Niagara*, Perry stubbornly continued the battle. He sailed through the very middle of the British squadron. The *Niagara's* cannons roared, smashing five of the enemy ships with cannonballs.

On September 10, 1813, Captain Oliver Hazard Perry fought the Battle of Lake Erie. When Perry's flagship the Lawrence *began to sink, Perry rowed to the* Niagara. *From this ship, he continued the fight and won a great victory.*

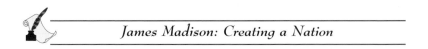

American soldiers commanded by General William Henry Harrison clashed with British and American Indian forces at the Battle of the Thames. In this bloody fight, the great Shawnee leader Tecumseh was killed.

After winning the battle, Perry sent out a famous message: "We have met the enemy and they are ours."[12]

Continued Fighting

Perry's stirring victory won the Americans total control of Lake Erie. Within days, General William Henry Harrison recaptured Fort Detroit. On October 5, Harrison's troops boarded Perry's ships and crossed into Ontario, Canada. At the Thames River, Harrison's army won a stunning victory against a force of British soldiers and their American Indian allies. During the Battle of the Thames, the great Shawnee leader and British ally Tecumseh was killed.

In November 1813, American General Andrew Jackson marched into present-day Alabama to fight an uprising of Creek Indians. Jackson's troops beat the Creek at the Battle of Horseshoe Bend in March 1814. American settlers were soon pouring into the conquered territory.

In the spring of 1814, Madison received surprising news from Europe. The British finally had won their war against the French. Madison realized that thousands of experienced British troops were now available to sail across the Atlantic. It seemed certain that the United States would soon face greater dangers than ever before.

Defeat and Victory

MADISON GUESSED THAT the British Navy would carry thousands of enemy troops from Europe to Chesapeake Bay, along the coast of Maryland and Virginia. Attorney General Richard Rush recalled that Madison believed "the capital would be marked as the most inviting object of a speedy attack."[1] Madison appointed General William Winder to command the defense of the region.

The British Invasion

In August, 1814, messengers galloped into Washington, D.C., with frightening news. A huge fleet of fifty-one British warships, commanded by Admiral George Cockburn, was indeed approaching the Maryland seacoast. It anchored at the mouth of the Patuxent River in Chesapeake Bay on August 18. Secretary of War John Armstrong refused to believe that the British planned to attack Washington, D.C. "Oh yes, by God," he declared, "they [mean] to strike somewhere, but they certainly will not come here; what the devil will they do here."[2]

Secretary of State James Monroe rode out with several cavalrymen to scout the situation. On the morning of August 20, Monroe stood on a little hill near Benedict, Maryland. Below him, he saw the landing of 4,500 British troops commanded by General Robert Ross. Ross's army began marching toward Bladensburg, Maryland, just six miles north of Washington, D.C.

Word of the British landing caused panic in Washington, D.C. People grabbed their children and valuables. They searched for wagons and carriages with which to escape the city. The clerks at the State Department gathered up important documents (including the Declaration of Independence). The papers were put in cloth bags and carried off to Leesburg, Virginia, for safekeeping. On August 22, one witness described the Washington panic in a letter:

> Women and children [are] running in every direction. . . . All is confusion. [Carriages and wagons] cannot be [gotten] for love or money. . . . I have just returned from taking a load of children eight miles out of town, and the whole distance the road was filled with women and children. Indeed I never saw so much distress in my life as today.[3]

A Visit to the Army

On August 22, 1814, Madison rode out to General Winder's headquarters at Long Old Fields, about eight miles east of Washington, D.C. Winder had gathered an army of three thousand troops. Several thousand more volunteers were on the way. But most of these soldiers had never been in battle before. They hardly knew how to fire their muskets.

On the morning of August 23, Madison reviewed the army. To Dolley, he scribbled a note. He told her that the soldiers who paraded before him had been "in high spirits & made a good appearance."[4] By the end of the day, General Winder ordered his army to march to Bladensburg. Madison rode back to the White House for the night.

General Ross's 4,500 British troops neared Bladensburg on the morning of August 24. As battle loomed, Madison rode back to the field to discuss plans with General Winder. He wrote a hurried note to his wife. She, in turn, wrote one to her sister, Lucy: "He desires I should be ready at a moment's warning to enter my carriage, and leave the city; that the enemy [seem] stronger than had been reported, and that it might happen that they would reach the city [and] destroy it." She explained that she had filled a carriage with government papers. But she refused to leave "until I see Mr. Madison safe, and he can accompany me."[5]

The Battle of Bladensburg

Before noon on August 24, 1814, the thermometer rose above 95 degrees Fahrenheit. In the heat, General Winder organized a hurried line of defense, as the British prepared to attack. Soon British Congreve rockets began screeching through the sky. They were like giant, noisy fire-crackers. Some of the terrifying rockets landed near Madison. He later remembered, "I observed to the Secretary of War and Secretary of State that it would be proper to withdraw to a position in the rear . . . leaving military movements to the military functionaries who were responsible for them."[6]

Madison and his cabinet rode farther to the rear of the battle. Before long, Madison received a hurried message from General Winder. His soldiers were being forced back. In fact, the American army was in full retreat. At the Battle of Bladensburg, the Americans panicked and ran, even though they outnumbered the British. In the fight, the British suffered about five hundred killed or wounded. The Americans suffered only about forty killed and sixty wounded. They had lost the battle simply because they had no experience and were easily frightened. Soon they were running in all directions.

The President in Retreat

At the White House, Dolley Madison at last climbed into a carriage. The coachman hurried for

Three o'clock. Will you believe it, my sister? We have had a battle or skirmish near Bladensburg, and I am still here within sound of the cannon! Mr. Madison comes not; may God protect him! Two messengers covered with dust, come bid me fly; but I wait for him. . . . At this late hour a wagon has been procurred, I have had it filled with the plate and most valuable portable articles belonging to the house. . . . Our kind friend, Mr. Carroll, has come to hasten my departure. . . . I insist on waiting until the large picture of Gen. Washington is [saved]. . . . I have ordered the frame to be broken, and the canvass taken out, it is done, and the precious portrait placed in the hands of two gentlemen of New York, for safe keeping. And now, dear sister, I must leave this house. . . . When I shall again write you, or where I shall be tomorrow, I cannot tell!![7]

On August 24, 1814, Dolley Madison wrote to her sister from the White House describing the Battle of Bladensburg.

the crowded bridge over the Potomac River into Virginia.

Madison reached the White House an hour later. He tried to reorganize some of the frightened soldiers who were streaming past the White House. But he soon saw it was hopeless. There was no one to defend the city from the advancing British. French Minister Louis Serurier recalled, "It was then . . . that the President . . . in the [middle] of all this disorder. . . . Coolly . . . mounted his horse, [and along with] some friends . . . slowly gained the bridge that separates Washington from Virginia."[8]

About six o'clock, Madison escaped into Virginia along with General John Mason and Attorney General Richard Rush. They spent the night at a house near Falls Church, Virginia. The next day, they tried to find what remained of General Winder's army. They rode back into Maryland and journeyed toward Baltimore.

The Burning of Washington

"You may thank old Madison for this," British Admiral George Cockburn declared to some citizens along the road from Bladensburg to Washington, D.C. "It is he who has got you into this scrape."[9] The British wanted revenge for the burning of York and other Canadian towns. Earlier, Cockburn had warned that it was his duty "to destroy and lay waste such towns and districts upon the coast as may be found available."[10]

As the sun set on August 24, General Ross and his British troops camped just outside Washington, D.C. He then marched a few hundred soldiers and sailors into the deserted city. The British reached the capitol about six o'clock. Some troops fired their muskets through the windows of the undefended building, breaking glass. General Ross then ordered torches lit. Pennsylvania Congressman Charles J. Ingersoll sadly recalled, the British left "the Capitol wrapped in [a] sheet of fire."[11]

By nine o'clock, a company of British sailors and marines marched into the yard of the White House. Admiral Cockburn had ridden along with these troops. Inside the deserted mansion, Cockburn picked up a few souvenirs. He kept an old hat of President Madison's and a cushion from one of Dolley Madison's chairs. Stepping outside again, he gave his orders. The sailors and marines smashed in the windows with their torches and set the White House on fire.

Other important buildings were also set on fire. They included the War Department and the Treasury Department buildings and the *National Intelligencer* newspaper office. A federal arsenal, where guns and ammunition were stored, was also soon in flames. British officer G. R. Gleig exclaimed, "The sky was brilliantly [lit] by the different [fires]; and a dark red light was thrown upon the road, [bright enough] to permit each man to [clearly see] his comrade's face."[12] Only a sudden rainstorm saved the entire city from burning to the ground.

British troops burned Washington, D.C., in 1814. This act was to avenge the burning of British towns in Canada earlier in the war.

On the morning of August 25, the British began the march back to Benedict, Maryland. They boarded their ships on August 30, 1814. Behind them, they left much of Washington, D.C., a heap of smoking ruins.

Out of the Ashes

Dolley Madison returned to the burned city on August 27. She found that nothing remained of the White House but blackened walls. She took shelter at her sister Anna's home, directly across F Street. Later that day, Madison finally joined her.

Madison was determined that the government continue. He ordered that the House of Representatives and the Senate meet in the Post Office and Patent buildings. Those two buildings had escaped the fires. French Minister Louis Serurier gave up his own home, the eight-sided Octagon House, for the Madisons to live in. The Madisons never again lived in the White House. By the time it was repaired in 1817, James Monroe was president.

Secretary of War Armstrong had done little to prepare for the British invasion. Under pressure from Madison, Armstrong soon resigned from office. Secretary of State Monroe took on the added duty of temporary secretary of war.

The Star Spangled Banner

Admiral Cockburn's British fleet sailed north. On September 11, 1814, General Ross's troops landed again. They stepped ashore fourteen miles below the port city of Baltimore, Maryland. Ross's soldiers marched toward Baltimore, which was protected by Fort McHenry. Along the road, an American sniper shot Ross from his horse and killed him. When the British attacked, they were beaten back by American militia commanded by General Samuel Smith.

"We'll take it in two hours," boasted Admiral Cockburn.[13] He still felt sure that Fort McHenry would surrender. For hours, the British fleet fired on the brick walls of the fort. Major George Armistead commanded Fort McHenry. He had ordered that a giant flag be raised "so large that the British will have no difficulty seeing it at a distance."[14] A young Maryland lawyer named Francis Scott Key watched the bombardment while aboard a British warship. Key was on board trying to gain the release of a captured American doctor. At dawn, Key saw through the smoke that the American flag still flew from Fort McHenry. The sight made him so proud he immediately wrote a poem to the music of a well-known song. It later became our national anthem, "The Star-Spangled Banner." In the end, the British retreated from Baltimore in defeat. The soldiers boarded the British ships and sailed out of Chesapeake Bay.

The Hartford Convention

In New York, the Americans won another stunning victory on September 11, 1814. At the Battle of Plattsburgh on Lake Champlain, Commodore Thomas McDonough captured four British warships.

Some New England Federalists, however, believed that the United States would lose the war. They called for a convention to force changes in the government. The danger of a nation split by politics in the middle of a war greatly worried Madison. Maryland citizen William Wirt visited the president at the end of September. In a letter to his wife, Wirt remarked, "He looks . . . shattered and wo-begone.

The Star-Spangled Banner

O say, can you see, by the dawn's early light,
What so proudly we hail'd at the twilight's last gleaming?
Whose broad stripes and bright stars, thro' the perilous fight,
O'er the ramparts we watch'd, were so gallantly streaming?
And the rockets' red glare, the bombs bursting in air,
Gave proof thro' the night that our flag was still there.
O say, does that star-spangled banner yet wave
O'er the land of the free and the home of the brave?[15]

The first verse of "The Star-Spangled Banner," a poem written by a Maryland lawyer named Francis Scott Key.

In short, he looked heart-broken. His mind is full of the New England [protest]."[16]

Twenty-seven Federalist delegates met in Hartford, Connecticut, on December 15. During their convention, they drew up a list of demands for amendments to the Constitution. One amendment limited presidents to a single term. Another amendment was aimed at Swiss-born Albert Gallatin whose treasury policies angered the Federalists. It would deny federal office to people born outside the United States. A third amendment was designed to keep Virginian James Monroe from becoming president after Madison. It insisted that no new president could be from the same state as the president before him. Three of the first four presidents had been Virginians. Many New Englanders insisted that Virginian control of the presidency had gone on for too long. By the time the Hartford Convention's demands were presented to Madison, however, the war had ended. They were never considered by Congress.

The Battle of New Orleans

"Turn your eyes to New Orleans!" exclaimed one newspaper.[17] It seemed certain that the British were planning to land an army to capture New Orleans. General Andrew Jackson hurried to New Orleans and prepared for its defense. Jackson gathered volunteer troops that included African Americans, Choctaw Indians, and French pirates. They piled bales of cotton along a New Orleans canal and waited behind them for the enemy attack.

On January 8, 1815, the British army marched into a hail of gunfire. In less than an hour, it was destroyed by Jackson's troops. The British suffered a shocking 2,600 killed, wounded, or captured. The cost to Jackson's army was only seven killed and six wounded. It was the greatest American victory of the war. The Battle of New Orleans made Andrew Jackson a national hero.

The Treaty of Ghent

Strangely, the Battle of New Orleans occurred after the War of 1812 had ended. At Ghent, Madison's peace commissioners had signed a treaty on December 24, 1814. The Treaty of Ghent arrived in Washington, D.C., on February 14. The Senate swiftly voted in favor of the treaty. On February 17, 1815, Madison proclaimed the war had ended. "The late war," Madison announced, "although reluctantly declared by congress . . . has been waged

During the Battle of New Orleans on January 8, 1815, American forces won a stunning victory over the British. They did not realize that the War of 1812 had already ended.

with a success, which is the natural result of the . . . patriotism of the people."[18] More than two thousand American troops had died fighting in the war. Over forty-five hundred had been wounded. The war had ended in a draw. No new territory had been won. No new promises between the two countries had been made. But it was certain that Great Britain would no longer impress American sailors.

Americans were proud of their success and praised Madison. The United States had fought the strongest nation in the world and had survived. The Richmond *Enquirer* exclaimed, "The sun never shone upon a people whose destinies promised to be grander."[19] Supreme Court Justice Joseph Story declared, "Peace has come in a most welcome time to delight and astonish us. Never did a country occupy more lofty ground; we have stood the contest, single-handed . . . and we are at peace, with all our blushing victories thick crowding on us."[20]

Final Years in Office

When they burned the Capitol, the British burned the Library of Congress. Madison soon afterward approved a new law allowing Congress to buy Thomas Jefferson's private book collection. Jefferson's books became the start of the nation's new library.

After the war, America's businesspeople and farmers returned to work. The national economy soon was booming. American shipyards echoed

Mr. Madison's administration has proved great points, long disputed in Europe and America:

1. He has proved that an administration, under our present Constitution, can declare war.
2. That it can make peace.
3. That . . . Great Britain can never conquer this country or any considerable part of it.
4. That our officers and men by land are equal to any [of Great Britain's forces].
5. That our navy is equal . . . to any that ever floated on the ocean.[21]

In a letter written in the summer of 1815, John Adams talked about James Madison's presidency.

with the noise of ships being built. Cargoes of trade goods were soon being shipped all over the world.

In 1816, James Monroe won the Republican nomination for president. He easily defeated the Federalist candidate, Rufus King, in the fall election. As Madison prepared to leave office, the United States entered a long period of economic success and national pride. "Never was a country left in a more flourishing situation," Albert Gallatin praised Madison, or its people "more united at home and respected abroad."[22]

The Father of the Constitution

"I AM IN THE MIDST OF preparations to get to my farm . . ." Madison told Albert Gallatin in the spring of 1817.[1] During his last days as president, Madison attended farewell parties and dinners. On April 6, he and Dolley at last left Washington, D.C., by steamboat. James K. Paulding, a fellow passenger, wrote, "If ever man sincerely rejoiced in being freed from the cares of public life, [it was Madison]. During the voyage he was as playful as a child; talked and joked with everybody on board, and reminded me of a schoolboy on a long vacation."[2] The steamboat docked at Aquia Creek, Virginia. There the Madisons met a carriage, which carried them the rest of the way to Montpelier.

Life at Montpelier

Madison was sixty-six years old when he retired to Montpelier. In retirement, he lived as an excellent farm manager and a happy host to guests.

Visiting friend Charles J. Ingersoll recalled the grounds and the house. "You enter his outer gate from the woods, and at once get into something like a park, with his . . . house about half a mile off."[3] British guest Harriet Martineau remembered, "The [house] stands on a gentle rise, and is neat and even handsome . . . with a flight of steps leading up to the portico."[4]

Curious strangers and old friends were always welcomed at Montpelier. On warm days, Dolley Madison sometimes spread dinner for as many as ninety guests at one time in the backyard. Margaret Bayard Smith visited Montpelier in 1828. Madison's conversation, she reported, was "a

In retirement, the Madisons welcomed a constant flow of guests to Montpelier. Visitors are still able to tour the estate today.

stream of history . . . rich in [feelings] and facts . . . it had an interest and charm, which the conversation of few men now living, could have. . . . His little blue eyes sparkled like stars from under his bushy gray eye-brows."[5] A young Harvard professor, George Ticknor, wrote during a visit:

Archaeology at Montpelier

Visitors are warmly welcomed at Montpelier today. They can tour the mansion, gaze at the grand mountain view from the portico, and stroll the green lawns and lovely garden. Archaeologists at Montpelier have discovered several sites of interest in recent years. Visitors can see remains of the mansion kitchen, slave quarters, and the slave burial ground. Near the Madison family cemetery, recent archaeological digging has revealed the site of the original Mount Pleasant homestead. Every summer, Montpelier's archaeologists continue their exciting investigations on the estate.

Montpelier

"Mr. Madison . . . is one of the most pleasant men I have met. . . . He lives, apparently, with great regularity. We breakfasted at nine, dined about four, drank tea at seven, and went to bed at ten . . . where Mrs. Madison sent us a nice supper every night."[6]

The Monroe Doctrine

Madison carefully read all of the newspapers and mail that arrived at Montpelier. Dolley Madison reported that he "passed part of every night in writing, reading and study."[7] Madison needed only a few hours of sleep each night. Beside his bed, he always kept a candle burning. Whenever he woke up, he often read or wrote.

James Monroe served two terms as President of the United States between 1817 and 1825. During that time, Madison often gave Monroe advice. In 1823, Monroe declared that European nations could no longer establish colonies in North and South America. If they tried, the United States felt that it had the right to declare war. Madison strongly agreed with this bold Monroe Doctrine.

The American Colonization Society

"Mr. Madison's farm," a visitor to Montpelier remembered, ". . . consists of about three thousand acres, with an hundred and eighty slaves, and is among the best managed in Virginia."[8] Madison did not think that black and whites could live peacefully together in freedom. He came to believe that sending freed slaves off to foreign colonies was the best solution to America's slavery problem.

In 1816, Madison helped organize the American Colonization Society. In 1821, the society founded Liberia in West Africa as a colony for former American slaves. The American Colonization Society sent about three thousand freed slaves to Liberia between 1821 and 1834. Madison, however, never freed his own slaves. He told Harriet Martineau, they had a "horror of going to Liberia."[9]

Madison had a plan for buying the freedom of America's entire slave population. The cost to pay for their freedom from their owners, he estimated, would be $600 million. Madison suggested that the United States sell 300 million acres of public land at two dollars an acre. But Congress failed to act on his idea.

Modern Farmer

Thomas Jefferson called Madison "the best farmer in the world."[10] In 1818, Madison was chosen as president of the Agricultural Society of Albemarle, which included five Virginia counties. Madison supported many new ideas for farming. He suggested that farmers plow their fields more deeply. He advised changing crops from time to time, using manure, and the careful breeding of cattle and sheep. He supported farming methods that would prevent the needless cutting down of trees and that would protect forests from fires. At Montpelier, Madison began raising sheep. Some of his slaves were set to work manufacturing cloth out of wool.

The University of Virginia

Thomas Jefferson designed the University of Virginia, which was founded in Charlottesville in 1819. The university accepted its first students in 1825. Jefferson died a year later, on July 4, 1826. Madison followed him as rector of the university. It was a position somewhat like university president. Each year, Madison traveled to Charlottesville to give students their examinations. One of these students was Edgar Allan Poe. Poe would later become one of America's greatest poets and short story writers. Among his famous writings are "The Raven" and "The Tell-Tale Heart."

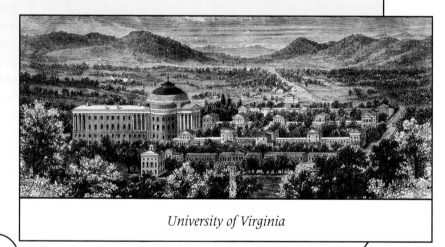

University of Virginia

The Father of the Constitution

On October 26, 1827, Charles J. Ingersoll delivered a toast at a dinner of Pennsylvania businessmen. "I offer . . ." he declared, "the health and happiness of James Madison, the father and guardian of the Constitution."[11] This was the first time Madison had been called the "Father of the Constitution." In response to a letter from William Cogswell, Madison wrote in 1831, "You give me credit to which I have no claim, in calling me 'the writer of the Constitution of the U.S.'" No single person was responsible for the document, Madison insisted. "It ought to be," he said, "regarded as the work of many heads & many hands."[12]

By the fall of 1829, Madison was the only signer of the Constitution still living. That year, Orange County voters elected him a delegate to a Virginia convention to revise the state's constitution. In Richmond, Madison shook hands with fellow delegates that included James Monroe and Chief Justice John Marshall.

In 1830, Vice President John C. Calhoun of South Carolina presented an argument that state laws could overturn national laws. From all sides, Madison received requests that he give his opinion on the subject. Madison published an article in the *North American Review* in October 1830. "The Constitution," he declared, "being a compact among the people of *all* the states, could not be altered or

By 1829, James Madison was the last signer of the Constitution still living. Already, Americans had started calling him the "Father of the Constitution."

annulled by the states individually." The Constitution, he added, was "the supreme law of the land."[13] States' rights would remain an issue of debate in the United States for the next thirty years. In the end, it would be a main cause of the Civil War, which began in 1861.

Crippling Disease

By 1831, Madison suffered from severe rheumatism, a joint disease that crippled his arms and legs. His fingers became so stiff, he could hardly write anymore. He explained to James Monroe, "the older I grow the more my stiffening fingers make smaller letters, as my feet take shorter steps."[14] By September 1831, Dolley remarked that her husband's illness, "has reduced him so much he can hardly walk from one bed to another."[15]

Madison also had a family problem that demanded his attention. His stepson, Payne Todd, was in constant debt because he was a gambler. To keep him out of prison, Madison eventually paid some $20,000 of his debts. An economic slump in Virginia added to Madison's problems. He was forced to sell part of his estate and, in 1834, sixteen of his slaves.

Harriet Martineau visited Madison in 1835. She found him crippled by rheumatism, deaf in one ear, and losing his sight, "his little person wrapped in a black silk gown, a warm gray and white cap upon his head . . ."[16] Though he remained in bed most of the time, Madison was "a wonderful man of

Defending the Constitution

Abraham Lincoln of Illinois was elected president in 1860. As a result of the general election it was also clear that antislavery northerners would take control of Congress in 1861. Many southerners feared that Lincoln would soon sign a national law doing away with slavery. Southerners who believed in states' rights vowed to protect their state slavery laws. In fact, by May 1861, eleven southern states had quit the Union and formed the Confederate States of America. President Lincoln and many northerners insisted that all the states had agreed forever to obey the Constitution when they ratified that document. The Civil War was fought to determine the issue. The South fought to gain independence and protect the principle of states' rights. The North battled to defend the Constitution and enforce the binding power of national law. After four years of bloody fighting, the South finally surrendered in 1865. The national government under the Constitution had been defended and preserved.

Abraham Lincoln

eighty-three. . . . His voice was clear and strong, and his manner of speaking particularly lively, often playful."[17] Sometimes when the Madisons had guests, he insisted his bedroom door be left open so he could hear the dining room conversation. Charles J. Ingersoll noted, "His understanding is as a bright as ever . . ."[18]

Death of a President

On June 28, 1836, one of Madison's nieces brought breakfast to Madison in bed. She soon noticed that he was having trouble swallowing.

"What is the matter, Uncle James?" she asked.

"Nothing more than a change of *mind*, my dear," he quietly answered.[19] Those were his last words.

"His head instantly dropped," described Madison's slave Paul Jennings, "and he ceased breathing as quietly as the snuff of a candle goes out."[20]

At the age of eighty-five, James Madison had died from heart failure. He was buried the next day in the family burial ground half a mile south of his house. "The last great light of the Revolution," mourned the *National Intelligencer*, "has at last sunk below the horizon."[21]

The First Lady

According to Madison's will, his library of books was left to the University of Virginia. He did not free his slaves, as he had wanted. He had realized that his wife would be left poor, if he did.

In 1837, Dolley Madison returned to live in Washington, D.C. Payne Todd was left in charge at Montpelier. He continued to gamble away his mother's property. Todd never sent his stepfather's books to the University of Virginia. He sold them instead.

In Washington, D.C., Dolley Madison spent the rest of her days a popular member of society. Her parties and dinners, as well as her son's wastefulness, cost her much. In 1837, she sold to Congress Madison's records of the Constitutional Convention for $30,000. Today, they remain the most important records of the Constitutional Convention. In the end, she also sold Montpelier to help pay her son's growing gambling debts. On July 12, 1849, Dolley Madison died at the age of eighty-one. She was buried in Washington, D.C. In 1858, her remains were taken to Montpelier and reburied next to her husband's. When she died, President Zachary Taylor declared, "She will never be forgotten because she was truly our First Lady for a half-century."[22] It was the first time a president's wife was called "The First Lady." The term has been used ever since.

Lasting Gifts to the Nation

Surely James Madison holds a place among the most important of the founding fathers. Thomas Jefferson called him "the greatest man in the world."[23] Madison's name will be forever linked with the birth and early growth of the United States.

During the American Revolution, Madison faithfully served in the Continental Congress. Winning independence, however, did not guarantee that the United States would survive. In 1787, the Constitution was written, guided by a plan designed by Madison. His essays in *The Federalist* helped persuade the states to approve the document. The Constitution became the solid set of laws from which the nation was able to grow. Madison then fought for the Bill of Rights, the first ten amendments to the Constitution. They guarantee all Americans many basic personal freedoms.

Madison went on to serve as a leader in Congress and as Thomas Jefferson's valued secretary of state. In 1808, his years of public service and patriotism earned him

James and Dolley Madison are buried in the family cemetery at Montpelier.

election as fourth President of the United States. To preserve America's rights at sea, Madison declared war against Great Britain in 1812.

By the time Madison died in 1836, the United States had already become a great nation. It could not have happened without Madison's help. In 1837, South Carolina Senator John C. Calhoun exclaimed, "We [are] indebted to Mr. Madison at least as much as to any other man, for the form of government under which we live."[24]

Timeline

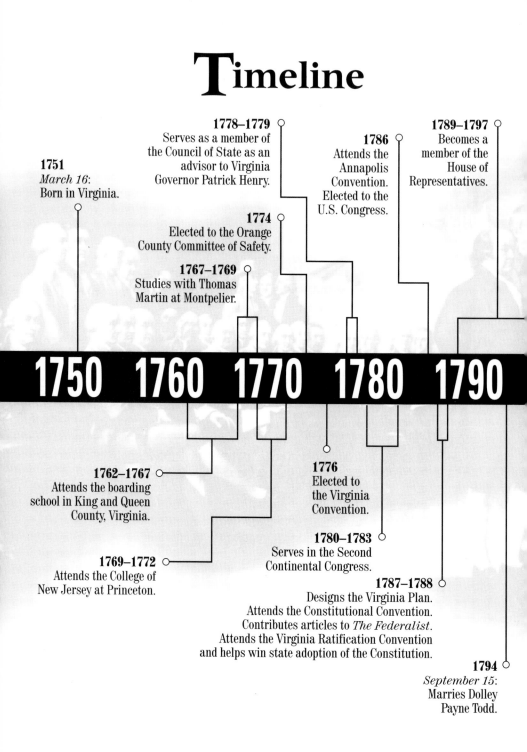

1751
March 16:
Born in Virginia.

1778–1779
Serves as a member of the Council of State as an advisor to Virginia Governor Patrick Henry.

1774
Elected to the Orange County Committee of Safety.

1767–1769
Studies with Thomas Martin at Montpelier.

1786
Attends the Annapolis Convention. Elected to the U.S. Congress.

1789–1797
Becomes a member of the House of Representatives.

1750 1760 1770 1780 1790

1762–1767
Attends the boarding school in King and Queen County, Virginia.

1769–1772
Attends the College of New Jersey at Princeton.

1776
Elected to the Virginia Convention.

1780–1783
Serves in the Second Continental Congress.

1787–1788
Designs the Virginia Plan.
Attends the Constitutional Convention.
Contributes articles to *The Federalist*.
Attends the Virginia Ratification Convention and helps win state adoption of the Constitution.

1794
September 15:
Marries Dolley Payne Todd.

1798
Writes Virginia Resolutions protesting the Alien and Sedition Acts.

1803
The United States buys the Louisiana Territory from Napoleon Bonaparte.

1808
Elected fourth President of the United States.

1811
The War Hawks urge war with Great Britain.

1813
September 10:
Oliver Hazard Perry defeats a British squadron at the Battle of Lake Erie.
October 5:
General William Henry Harrison defeats a force of British and American Indians at the Battle of the Thames.

1815
January 8:
Americans win a stunning victory over the British at the Battle of New Orleans.

1836
June 28:
Dies of heart failure at the age of eighty-five.

1800 1810 1820 1830 1840

1801–1809
Serves as secretary of state.

1807
June 22:
The British warship *Leopard* attacks the American warship *Chesapeake*.

1810
October 27:
Annexes West Florida territory.

1812
June 18:
United States declares war against Great Britain.
August 16:
General William Hull surrenders Fort Detroit.
August 19:
The U.S.S. *Constitution* defeats the British warship *Guerriére*.
Fall:
Madison wins a second term as president in the fall election.

1814
August 20:
British troops land in Maryland.
August 24:
Americans lose the Battle of Bladensburg.
September:
British defeated in attempt to capture Baltimore.
December 24:
The Treaty of Ghent is signed.

1826
Serves as rector of the University of Virginia.

Chapter Notes

Chapter 1. The Fight for the Constitution

1. Catherine Drinker Bowen, *Miracle at Philadelphia* (Boston: Little, Brown and Company, 1966), p. 293.

2. Irving Brant, *The Fourth President, A Life of James Madison* (Indianapolis: The Bobbs-Merrill Company, 1970), p. 31.

3. Bowen, p. 298.

4. Brant, p. 220.

5. Ibid., p. 210.

6. Merrill D. Peterson, ed., *The Founding Fathers, James Madison, A Biography in His Own Words* (New York: Newsweek Books, 1974), Vol. 1, p. 157.

7. Brant, p. 218.

8. Ibid., p. 217.

9. Ibid., p. 221.

10. William A. DeGregorio, *The Complete Book of U.S. Presidents* (New York: Dembner Books, 1984), p. 69.

Chapter 2. Young Revolutionary

1. William A. DeGregorio, *The Complete Book of U.S. Presidents* (New York: Dembner Books, 1984), p. 57.

2. Robert A. Rutland, *James Madison and the Search for Nationhood* (Washington, D.C.: The Library of Congress, 1981), p. 18.

3. Ibid., pp. 17, 18.

4. Garry Wills, *James Madison* (New York: Henry Holt and Company, 2002), p. 6.

5. Irving Brant, *The Fourth President, A Life of James Madison* (Indianapolis: The Bobbs-Merrill Company, 1970), p. 23.

6. Merrill D. Peterson, ed., *The Founding Fathers, James Madison, A Biography in His Own Words* (New York: Newsweek Books, 1974), Vol. 1, p. 34.

7. Rutland, p. 20.

8. Brant, p. 27.

9. Ibid., p. 35.

10. Wills, p. 17.

11. Brant, p. 31.

12. Harold S. Schultz, *James Madison* (New York: Twayne Publishers, Inc., 1970), p. 31.

13. Brant, p. 40.

14. Peterson, p. 48.

15. DeGregorio, p. 69.

16. Brant, p. 67.

17. Ibid., p. 109.

18. Ibid., p. 49.

19. Ibid., pp. 112–113.

20. Ibid.

21. Peterson, p. 81.

22. Brant, p. 120.

23. Ibid., p. 134.

24. Catherine Drinker Bowen, *Miracle at Philadelphia* (Boston: Little, Brown and Company, 1966), p. 33.

Chapter 3. Designing a National Government

1. Merrill D. Peterson, ed., *The Founding Fathers, James Madison, A Biography in His Own Words* (New York: Newsweek Books, 1974), Vol. 1, p. 102.

2. Ibid., p. 132.

3. Catherine Drinker Bowen, *Miracle at Philadelphia* (Boston: Little, Brown and Company, 1966), p. 30.

4. Irving Brant, *The Fourth President, A Life of James Madison* (Indianapolis: The Bobbs-Merrill Company, 1970), p. 147.

5. Bowen, p. 62.

6. Henry Steele Commager, "The Constitution: Was It an Economic Document?" *American Heritage*, December 1958, p. 58.

7. Kenneth W. Leish, ed., *The American Heritage Pictorial History of the Presidents of the United States* (New York: American Heritage Publishing Co., Inc., 1968), Vol. I, p. 130.

8. Robert A. Rutland, *James Madison and the Search for Nationhood* (Washington, D.C.: The Library of Congress, 1981), 56.

9. Paul F. Boller, Jr., *Presidential Anecdotes* (New York: Penguin Books, 1981), p. 45.

10. Brant, p. 179.

11. The United States Constitution.

12. Brant, p. 192.

13. Bowen, p. 256.

14. Ibid., p. 263.

Chapter 4. United States Congressman

1. Catherine Drinker Bowen, *Miracle at Philadelphia* (Boston: Little, Brown and Company, 1966), p. 213.

2. Ibid., p. 278.

3. Ibid., p. 281.

4. Garry Wills, *James Madison* (New York: Henry Holt and Company, 2002), p. 30.

5. Irving Brant, *The Fourth President, A Life of James Madison* (Indianapolis: The Bobbs-Merrill Company, 1970), p. 203.

6. Robert A. Rutland, *James Madison and the Search for Nationhood* (Washington, D.C.: The Library of Congress, 1981), p. 69.

7. William A. DeGregorio, *The Complete Book of the Presidents* (New York: Dembner Books, 1984), p. 60.

8. William F. Swindler, "The Letters of Publius," *American Heritage*, June 1961, p. 93.

9. Harold S. Schultz, *James Madison* (New York: Twayne Publishers, Inc. 1970), p. 88.

10. Brant, p. 226.

11. Ibid., p. 230.

12. Ibid., p. 224.

13. Rutland, p. 92.

14. Brant, p. 278.

15. Merrill D. Peterson, ed., *The Founding Fathers, James Madison, A Biography in His Own Words* (New York: Newsweek Books, 1974), Vol. 2, p. 221.

16. Ibid., p. 225.

Chapter 5. Secretary of State

1. Merrill D. Peterson, ed., *The Founding Fathers, James Madison, A Biography in His Own Words* (New York: Newsweek Books, 1974), Vol. 2, p. 246.

2. Ibid., p. 248.

3. Ibid.

4. Ibid.

5. Irving Brant, *The Fourth President, A Life of James Madison* (Indianapolis: The Bobbs-Merrill Company, 1970), p. 345.

6. David McCullough, *John Adams* (New York: Simon & Schuster, 2001), pp. 406–407.

7. Peterson, pp. 250–251.

8. Brant, p. 343.

9. Ibid., p. 346.

10. Peterson, p. 262.

11. Robert A. Rutland, *James Madison and the Search for Nationhood* (Washington, D.C.: The Library of Congress, 1981), pp. 75–76.

12. Peterson, p. 216.

13. Brant, p. 392.

14. Harold S. Schultz, *James Madison* (New York: Twayne Publishers, Inc. 1970), p. 145.

15. Brant, p. 399.

Chapter 6. The Fourth President

1. Merrill D. Peterson, ed., *The Founding Fathers, James Madison, A Biography in His Own Words* (New York: Newsweek Books, 1974), p. 274.

2. Harold S. Schultz, *James Madison* (New York: Twayne Publishers, Inc. 1970), pp. 147–148.

3. Peterson, p. 273.

4. Ibid., p. 275.

5. Paul F. Boller, Jr., *Presidential Anecdotes* (New York: Penguin Books, 1981), pp. 46–47.

6. Irving Brant, *The Fourth President, A Life of James Madison* (Indianapolis: The Bobbs-Merrill Company, 1970), p. 408.

7. Kenneth W. Leish, ed., *The American Heritage Pictorial History of the Presidents of the United States* (New York: American Heritage Publishing Co., Inc., 1968), Vol. I, p. 131.

8. Brant, p. 461.

9. Ibid., p. 467.

10. Schultz, p. 154.

11. Robert A. Rutland, *James Madison and the Search for Nationhood* (Washington, D.C.: The Library of Congress, 1981), p. 117.

12. Leish, Vol. I, p. 132.

13. Rutland, p. 119.

14. Peterson, p. 298.

Chapter 7. Mr. Madison's War

1. Irving Brant, *The Fourth President, A Life of James Madison* (Indianapolis: The Bobbs-Merrill Company, 1970), p. 497.

2. Kenneth W. Leish, ed., *The American Heritage Pictorial History of the Presidents of the United States* (New York: American Heritage Publishing Co., Inc., 1968), Vol. I, p. 132.

3. Paul F. Boller, Jr., *Presidential Anecdotes* (New York: Penguin Books, 1981), p. 46.

4. Leish, Vol. I, p. 132.

5. Garry Wills, *James Madison* (New York: Henry Holt and Company, 2002), p. 115.

6. Brant, p. 487.

7. Paul F. Boller, Jr., *Presidential Campaigns* (New York: Oxford University Press, 1984), p. 27.

8. William A. DeGregorio, *The Complete Book of U.S. Presidents* (New York: Dembner Books, 1984), p. 63.

9. Brant, p. 529.

10. Ibid., p. 535.

11. Wills, p. 122.

12. DeGregorio, p. 66.

Chapter 8. Defeat and Victory

1. Irving Brant, *The Fourth President, A Life of James Madison* (Indianapolis: The Bobbs-Merrill Company, 1970), p. 566.

2. Ibid., p. 568.

3. Willis Thornton, "The Day They Burned the Capitol," *American Heritage*, December 1954, p. 50.

4. Harold S. Schultz, *James Madison* (New York: Twayne Publishers, Inc. 1970), p. 179.

5. Brant, *The Fourth President, A Life of James Madison*, pp. 569–570.

6. Ibid., p. 572.

7. Merrill D. Peterson, ed., *The Founding Fathers, James Madison, A Biography in His Own Words* (New York: Newsweek Books, 1974), pp. 346–347.

8. Irving Brant, "Timid President? Futile War?" *American Heritage*, October 1959, p. 89.

9. Peterson, p. 315.

10. Brant, *The Fourth President, A Life of James Madison*, p. 578.

11. Kenneth W. Leish, ed., *The American Heritage Pictorial History of the Presidents of the United States* (New York: American Heritage Publishing Co., Inc., 1968), Vol. I, p. 144.

12. Thornton, p. 52.

13. Brant, *The Fourth President, A Life of James Madison,* p. 579.

14. Robert A. Rutland, *James Madison and the Search for Nationhood* (Washington, D.C.: The Library of Congress, 1981), p. 150.

15. Mark S. Hoffman, ed., *The World Almanac and Book of Facts 1993* (New York: World Almanac, 1993), p. 545.

16. Schultz, p. 15.

17. Brant, *The Fourth President, A Life of James Madison,* p. 586.

18. Peterson, pp. 354–355.

19. Rutland, p. 124.

20. Garry Wills, *James Madison* (New York: Times Books Henry Holt and Company, 2002), p. 158.

21. Ibid., p. 157.

22. Peterson, p. 364.

Chapter 9. The Father of the Constitution

1. Merrill D. Peterson, ed., *The Founding Fathers, James Madison, A Biography in His Own Words* (New York: Newsweek Books, 1974), p. 364.

2. Irving Brant, *The Fourth President, A Life of James Madison* (Indianapolis: The Bobbs-Merrill Company, 1970), p. 607.

3. Harold S. Schultz, *James Madison* (New York: Twayne Publishers, Inc. 1970), pp. 202–203.

4. Ibid., p. 203.

5. Paul F. Boller, Jr., *Presidential Anecdotes* (New York: Penguin Books, 1981), p. 47.

6. Peterson, pp. 367–368.

7. Schultz, p. 17.

8. Peterson, pp. 367–368.

9. Schultz, pp. 196–197.

10. David C. Whitney, *The American Presidents* (New York: Doubleday & Company, 1967), p. 43.

11. Brant, p. 622.

12. Schultz, p. 77.
13. Brant, p. 627.
14. Ibid., p. 629.
15. Ibid., p. 630.
16. Peterson, p. 377.
17. Brant, p. 637.
18. Ibid., p. 640.
19. Peterson, p. 405.
20. Ibid.
21. Brant, p. 642.

22. Peyton Lewis, "Discovering Dolley," *Discovering Montpelier*, Winter 2003, p. 11.

23. Robert A. Rutland, *James Madison and the Search for Nationhood* (Washington, D.C.: The Library of Congress, 1981), p. 3.

24. Schultz, p. 5.

Glossary

amend—To change, put right, or improve.

bales—Large, closely pressed packages.

boycott—To refuse to buy or sell goods from a specific person, store, organization, or country.

census—A count of the population.

commerce—The buying or selling of goods.

diplomat—A person skilled as a representative to a foreign nation.

Electoral College—A body of people chosen to decide an election.

embargo—A government order prohibiting commerce with an enemy.

feud—A continuing argument, sometimes violent.

hull—The frame or body of a ship.

legislature—A group of people with the power to make laws.

musket—A gun with a long barrel that is smooth on the inside.

ratify—To approve formally.

resolution—The call for an expression of opinion by a governing body.

sniper—One who shoots from a hidden position.

squadron—A group of two or more ships or airplanes.

turban—A headdress of cloth that is worn wrapped around the head.

Further Reading

Books

Collier, Christopher and James Lincoln Collier. *Creating the Constitution: 1787*. Tarrytown, N.Y.: Marshall Cavendish Corporation, 1999.

Leebrick, Kristal. *The Constitution*. Mankato, Minn.: Capstone Press, Inc., 2002.

Marcovitz, Hal. *The Declaration of Independence*. Broomall, Pa.: Mason Crest Publishers, 2002.

Pflueger, Lynda. *Dolley Madison: Courageous First Lady*. Berkeley Heights, N.J.: Enslow Publishers, 1999.

Strelloff, Rebecca. *The War of 1812*. Tarrytown, N.Y.: Marshall Cavendish, 2001.

Internet Addresses

Interesting.com. "The Federalist Papers."
FoundingFathers.info. © 2001–2002. <http://www.
foundingfathers.info/federalistpapers/>.

James Madison's Montpelier. "Kids Corner." n.d.
<http://www.montpelier.org/kids.htm>.

Kidsnewsroom.org. "James Madison: Fourth President
of the United States, 1809–1817." *United States
Presidents.* 1997. <http://kidsnewsroom.com/elmer/
infocentral/frameset/presidents/>.

Places to Visit

Federal Hall National Memorial
    26 Wall Street
    New York, New York 10005
    (212) 825-6888
    <http://www.nps.gov/feha/>

Independence National Historical Park
    143 South Third Street
    Philadelphia, Pennsylvania 19106
    (215) 597-8974
    <http://www.nps.gov/inde/>

James Madison's Montpelier
    11407 Constitution Highway
    Montpelier Station, Virginia 22957
    (540) 672-2728
    <http://www.montpelier.org>

The White House
    1600 Pennsylvania Avenue
    Washington, D.C.
    (202) 456-7041
    <http://www.whitehouse.gov/>

Index